NAKED EDUCATION

BOOK 2

THE ROLE OF CONSCIOUSNESS IN THEORY AND PRACTICE

Toni and Jay Garland

Editing by Tad Wilson

Cover illustration by Karin Wells

Formatting by Debora Lewis arenapublishing.org

ISBN: 978-0-9985869-1-5

Books in the Naked Education Series
by Jay and Toni Garland

Author contact information: If any of the readers of the series wish to communicate with Jay or Toni, or both, either to suggest corrections to the text, or to comment in any way about any of the books in the series, to make suggestions, to ask questions, or to start a new conversation, our e-mail addresses are jay@jtgarland.com or toni@jtgarland.com or authors@jtgarland.com. Or read our blog: http://newearthinstitute.blogspot.com/2010/03/jay-and-toni-garland-bio.html. If anyone would like assistance in starting a school, the authors will do what they can to assist, including traveling to where a group of founders and innovators live to meet with you and discuss the methods of Naked Education.

CONTENTS

Acknowledgments

It seemed to Jay and Toni Garland that a host of angels, some from the spiritual world and some in the flesh, guided them in founding The Well School in 1967, especially Peter Garland who invited his brother and sister-in-law to move from Pilot Station, Alaska and start a school in Peterborough, New Hampshire. We especially appreciate those first families that trusted Jay and Toni to develop a school that fed the souls of their children: Peter and Mary Garland, Arthur and R.M. Eldredge, Bill and Liz Bowen. Their enthusiasm made starting the school a thrilling adventure.

We took nearly 15 years to write and publish this book as a paperback, due in part to the need for recuperation after Jay Garland has a debilitating stroke in 2005, and open heart bypass surgery in 2013.

We are extremely appreciative for "Tad," Artelia Lyn Ellis (Wilson,) a former Well School student for her comprehensive edit. Her first-hand knowledge of the school as a student at The Well School adds an additional dimension to her work. And her poem at the end of Book 1 adds both significance and insight about her experience.

And, thank you Tim Lowry, for sharing your love of poetry, for the poetry and the quotes clarify many points concerning the "ineffable." Your editing comments led to increased clarity of our message.

A dear friend and former parent at The Well School, Karin Wells, suggested that we buy an Apple computer and publish our manuscripts on iBooks after she had published 8 iBooks of her own. She guided the Garlands through every step of the process of self-publishing, never doubting their ability to learn the ropes. Karin is responsible for designing the book covers as well, each of which displays wonderful Well School student art.

Our thanks to Cassandra Leoncini for accomplishing, after all these years, the final edit that contains significant changes. Cassandra had no connection to The Well School, so provided an objective view from outside. And thanks to Debora Lewis for formatting this book so that it could be printed by CreateSpace.

Introduction: What is "Naked Education?"

"Naked Education" is a radical form of organic education. The root of "Naked Education" is and was the vision given to Toni & Jay Garland, the authors of this book and the founders of The Well School in Peterborough, New Hampshire in 1967. For thirty-five years, they served as directors and full-time teachers as they were led to evolve and implement this new form of education.

Toni and Jay received an invaluable education while teaching four years in two Inuit (Eskimo) villages in Alaska. The Inuit exposed them to the love, joy, and intimacy of true community in which all the villagers take responsibility for one another and all adults take responsibility for the young. The Inuit demonstrated to the Garlands the principle of Inclusion – all are included, none excluded. This principle guided the Garlands during their tenure at The Well School.

Naked Education metaphorically envisions the nature of the soul of every child. Metaphorically, young children still live in the Garden of Eden. It is obvious that they are still connected to Spirit and possess the many qualities of Spirit: Innocence, Unconditional Love, Peace, the Life Force, Inner Wisdom, Intuition, Creativity, Freedom, Joy, Spontaneity, Curiosity, Generosity, Luminosity, and Imagination.

"What?" you say, "I've never seen children demonstrate those qualities! In fact, the children I've known are quite the opposite, and need a regimen of strict training, instruction, and discipline in order to become civilized! That's the job of parents and schools! That's why in our society we have laws and institutions! If we didn't routinely punish bad behavior and serve as role models of good behavior, we'd live in chaos and anarchy. That's why we have schools and reform schools and the police and the military."

The perspective of Naked Education challenges that position. It assumes that originally we were created in the image of our Creator with all the positive attributes listed above. That original nature of our Soul is still alive and well within us, forever connected with Spirit, even when we deny it or are not conscious of this connection.

Yet the interplay with our environment creates a second self with which we readily identify. Many call it our "self" or our "identity" or our "ego," or "coyote trickster," or our "ego consciousness." Whatever we call it, it represents the part of us that is conditioned by the beliefs of others, most notably by the beliefs of our parents or caregivers, our friends, and our teachers. The identity of our ego includes our name, our physical body, our behavior, our personality, our thoughts, and our emotions. We have an unspoken agreement that what each of us identify with is who we are.

This dual identity of Soul and ego, our real Self and our imagined self need further clarification. Our ego's goals in life can be contrasted with our Soul's purpose, states Eli Jaxon-Bear, born in Brooklyn, New York, but trained in India by his spiritual teacher, Papaji:

> *The soul's awakening is the purpose of life. It awakens from its identification with form and consciously returns to its union with God. The soul incarnates by identifying with its denser form, the condensation out of emptiness.*

> ~Eli Jaxon-Bear, *Sudden Awakening* [1]

The soul produces from within itself ever-denser forms, including the human body. Ego identification with the body mirrors the soul, but it calls itself "I."

These two identities, Soul and ego, are also represented in two passages of the *Holy Bible* in Genesis that sit in close proximity. The first passage (Genesis, chapter 1, verse 27, King James translation) says, "God created man in his own likeness and image, in the image of God created he him; male and female created he them." Does that not suggest, from the beginning the essence of man – his Soul – replicates the essence of his Creator? Except for the distinction that God created man and not the other way around, man and the inner God are unified, perhaps even potentially creative partners.

Occasionally I, Jay Garland, mention "God" in this series of six books. My understanding of God is, no doubt, different from yours. For me, "God" lives within, for "God" is our highest consciousness. Every time our consciousness expands significantly, or our identity enlarges, our exterior reality shifts to conform to how we now view ourselves. We never exhaust our capacity to ascend in consciousness; it's an endless process. So there are not ultimate masters or quintessential gurus. Even Jesus taught that others also potentially have the power that he demonstrated.

> *Verily, verily, I say unto you, He that believeth on me, the works that I do shall he do also; and greater works than these he shall do, for I go unto my Father.*

> ~*Holy Bible:* John 14:12; [2]

God, in our world is a concept that often divides us into separate religions, rather than unites us into one people. Although the connection between Khwāja Shams-ud-Dīn Muammad āfe-e Shīrāzī, a Persian poet from the 14th century, and twentieth century Naked Education appears remote, Hafiz in the following poem, captures the essence and spirit of Naked Education succinctly. Hafiz makes no stilted reference to religious doctrine or Biblical quotes, emphasizing instead the spirit of play, freedom, joy, and love that colored so many Well School daily activities:

I have learned so much from God

> *I have learned so much from God that I can no longer*
> *call myself a Christian, a Hindu, A Muslim, A Buddhist, A Jew.*
> *The Truth has shared so much of itself with me that*
> *I can no longer call myself a man, a woman, an angel, or even pure soul.*
> *Love has befriended Hafiz so completely that it has turned to ash*
> *and freed me of every concept and image my mind has ever known.*

~Hafiz [4]

I understand *The Bible* as the greatest psychological book written. I do not see it as a history of certain historical personalities. *The Bible,* if interpreted psychologically and metaphorically, describes some aspect of ourself in every story it tells; sometimes it describes many aspects of our nature in the drama of a single story. All the characters in a story are aspects of ourself, aspects of our consciousness. The same is true of the Bhagavad Gita and many ancient eastern sacred texts.For me, God also refers to selfless Love. The formless energy that runs through everything has these characteristics: Intelligence, Beauty, Creativity, Peace, Love, Emptiness, Eternalness, and the state of Freedom.

And the belief in masters and gurus is a confession of the believer's slavery. For only slaves have masters. But a change in one's identity transforms one totally as it transforms one's world. No gods or masters required!

The second account of creation from the *Holy Bible* is radically different. Instead of emphasizing unity, its perspective is duality, hierarchy, disobedience, sin, and punishment. It is the story of the separation from God by man. God fashioned man from the "dust of the ground and breathed into his nostrils the breath of life; and man became a living soul." Shortly after, God creates Eve from one of Adam's ribs. God instructs Adam and Eve to eat the fruit of every tree EXCEPT the Tree of the Knowledge of Good and Evil lest they die. It is clearly stated at the very end of chapter 2 that "they were both naked, and were not ashamed."

Chapter 3 of Genesis goes on to tell the seminal story of our culture – the bitter separation of God and man. Enter the serpent. It questions the connection that God has made between eating fruit of the Tree of Knowledge of Good and Evil and *Death*, claiming that eating this fruit will not cause death, but wisdom.

As soon as they both do eat the prohibited fruit, they are traumatized. "Their eyes were opened and they knew they were naked." Instinctively "they sewed fig leaves together, and made themselves an apron" to cover their private parts. When they commit the forbidden act, they immediately become self-conscious and guilty. As a result of their disobedience, God drives them from the Garden of Eden lest they eat from the Tree of Life and live forever, and He stations angels with swords around the garden so that they can never return to God's paradise. God also curses their lives, including a life of futile toil for Adam and painful childbirth for Eve. This story is a rationalization – both an explanation and a justification – of how duality and a toilsome life filled with suffering replaces the original unity between God and man. It highlights how deceit and disobedience are so repugnant to God that He separates himself from man and damns him. It is the story of Paradise Lost.

This second story is often summarized by the phrase, "original sin." Viewed from the perspective of Naked Education, the belief in sin is a descent into lower consciousness. This "fall of man" represents a reality that many of us accept as ultimately true – that we are separate entities, disconnected from Soul and Spirit, other people, and all other life forms. It is a viewpoint that we are ultimately competitors, rivals for attention and praise.

Ego vacillates between seeing itself in grandiose or heroic terms, or, in contrast, as a puny victim – vulnerable, subject to bad luck, abuses, illnesses and death. In either case, ego insists on its separation from Spirit for its very existence *requires alienation*.

The transformation from innocence and wellbeing to guilt and shame appears immediately when we view life through ego's eyes. Yet when we cease to believe ego's voice of fear and guilt, we immediately return to paradise and reawaken to all our blessings.

Naked Education refutes the notion that children are born in sin. Nor are children ignorant beings in need of training and instruction. Instead it sees children in their original "naked" state – loving, innocent, creative beings, whose true nature is love, spontaneity, creativity, intuition, and joy. Naked Education consistently empowers children to discover and reveal their innate intelligence and genius.

Naked Education is not derivative. Its fundamental assumptions are not taught in any teachers' college. It does not subscribe to the notion that students must pass certain tests before they can do things that are fun, or that teachers cannot teach until they first receive specific training at a teachers' college. Nor does it insist that students curb their enthusiasm or conform to some predetermined ideal. And finally, it does not prepare children for some future job that may or may not exist in the future. Naked Education has one simple goal: for children to know through experience their true Self. How is this done? By helping students connect to their innate, individual genius, and by providing a wide range of activities that allow kids to joyfully express themselves. Naked Education explores this in great depth.

The Kahlil Gibran poem, "On Children," from his book, *The Prophet*, appearing below, captures this original, sacred nature of children; to become fully empowered beings means to return to one's inscrutable, true being.

On Children

> *Your children are not your children.*
> *They are the sons and daughters of Life's longing for itself.*
> *They come through you but not from you,*
> *And though they are with you, yet they belong not to you.*
> *You may give them your love, but not your thoughts,*
> *For they have their own thoughts.*
> *You may house their bodies but not their souls,*
> *For their souls dwell in the house of tomorrow, which you cannot visit, not even in your dreams.*
> *You may strive to be like them, but seek not to make them like you.*
> *For life goes not backward nor tarries with yesterday.*
> *You are the bows from which your children as living arrows are sent forth.*
> *The archer sees the mark upon the path of the infinite, and He bends you with His might that His arrows may go swift and far.*
> *Let your bending in the archer's hand be for gladness;*
> *For even as He loves the arrow that flies,*
> *so He loves also the bow that is stable.*
>
> ~Khalil Gibran, *The Prophet* [3]

I love poetry for its ability to point to the ineffable, its propensity to illuminate, to cast light on a subject, to reveal beauty and truth. Whereas prose is suited to discussion of the material world and the logical, conceptual thinking used to understand that world, poetry is the perfect medium to express feeling, sensation, and intuition. Prose captures physical reality; poetry limns beauty, potential, and creative possibility.

I love this particular Gibran poem, for its ability to contrast the parent that unconditionally loves his child with the parent that views his child as an extension of himself. The first parent experiences awe in the presence of his child; he acknowledges that his offspring will experience a broader reality. The second parent seeks to make his child a reflection of himself because he views the child as his property – he sees his child as his to mold and takes personal pride in his progeny's accomplishments.

These two perspectives on children reveal two different states of consciousness that parents express: the lover and the owner. At the same time parents have a crucial choice to make: How do I want to envision my child? The rub is that this choice implies a second choice: How do I want to envision my role as parent?

Parent #1 recognizes her child as human, yet as a precious, Divine gift with individual purpose, singular destiny, and distinctive talents and potentials. She unconditionally loves her offspring. Parent #2 has an altogether different perspective. Her covert intention is *to train* "her" child with rewards and punishments in order to make her son or daughter "good," worthy of love, so that he or she does not become "naughty" or "bad," worthy of contempt.

Gibran shows us that an enormous chasm exists between these two views, for the poem implies two scenarios, two distinct possibilities for parent and child. The first implies light, growth and freedom for both parent and child. The second portends a power struggle between the authority and the underling. Within a family, the consequences of adopting one or the other of Kahlil Gibran's takes on parents and children are substantial and far-reaching. They, in no small way, determine the dynamics between parents and children.

As with parent and child, so also with schools and students. A similar "Grand Canyon" of perspective and perception separates how schools perceive their students. Do schools exist to awaken students to their idiosyncratic, unique, and glorious potential, or do they represent a system of indoctrination to ensure that students conform to "standards of excellence" as defined by educational officials? Do school systems view children as possessing genius or do they interpret them as empty, ignorant vessels to be filled with knowledge by their "educated" parents and teachers? By "genius" I mean intelligence and creative brilliance in some aspects of life. Our particular genius reveals our vast greatness and prompts us to fulfill our life purpose through following what gives us joy.

Naked Education assumes that authentic parents and authentic teachers "are the bows from which your children as living arrows are sent forth" and that authentic schools exist to empower children. The Well School has been a manifestation of the vision that children, parents, and teachers can work together to create a *community* devoted to allowing genius and love to flourish. All is possible in an environment where beauty, truth, and individual expression are honored.

Similarly, a school's perception of what children in essence are, has extraordinary implications for children, parents, teachers, and for the nature of a society. The consciousness of all players in the educational system is drastically changed by adopting one view or the other. Today the preferred education is the industrial, factory-style, assembly-line system intended to create uniform products: those who have successfully ingested and regurgitated the educational canon. This education of conformity reaches from kindergarten to colleges and universities.

Naked Education, in contrast, is soul education, heart education, and loving education attuned to inner intuition. The curriculum is whatever feeds the soul and heart at the center of our being, whatever empowers us, whatever reveals our essence: love, joy, light, curiosity, and invention. The purpose of life is to awaken us so that we can learn how to live in harmony with Self, others, and the outside world; the purpose is to discover what we love, what makes us happy, so we may practice it again and again throughout our lifetime. We are not here to feed our ego or control others! We are here to experience the freedom and joy that evolves from loving our life and everyone in our life.

Naked Education resonates with the sayings of Jesus found in the *Gospel of Thomas*, discovered in 1945, a "lost" gospel that predates the Biblical canonical gospels sanctioned by the Catholic Church at the First Council of Nicaea in AD 325. *The Gospel of Thomas*, composed of only 140 sayings of Jesus, is the earliest of all known gospels, and rejects later notions constructed by the Catholic Church, including the Christian doctrines of Crucifixion, Resurrection, Sin, and Salvation. The Gospel of Thomas says that Heaven is available now – not after the body dies. It stresses that one must *rely on one's intuition* to answer significant questions that are asked in Thomas' gospel before the meaning of the sayings becomes illuminated within.

The Gospel of Thomas [17] like Naked Education, emphasizes positive human nature and everyone's capacity to know themselves *without the help of outside agents* – including one's parents, one's religious institution, or one's guru. The first two sayings in this gospel are: *"And he said: Whoever finds the correct interpretation of these sayings will never die,"* And Jesus said, *"The seeker should not stop until he finds. When he does find, he will be disturbed. After having been disturbed he will be astonished. Then he will reign over everything."*

Saying 3 asserts, *When you understand yourselves, you will be understood. And you will realize that you are sons of the living Father. If you do not know yourselves, then you exist in poverty and you are that poverty."*

In saying 14A, Jesus said to them: *"If you fast you will bring sin to yourself, and if you pray, you will be condemned, and if you give to charity you will damage your spirits."* Fasting, praying, and charitable giving make the *ego* appear virtuous and so are not applicable to spiritual life. Inner discerning and knowing is reflected in how one sees inner and outer reality and is the secret of *The Gospel of Thomas* as well as the secret of Naked Education.

We Have Not Come Here to Take Prisoners

We have not come here to take prisoners,
But to surrender ever more deeply to freedom and joy.
We have not come into this exquisite world
To hold ourselves hostage from love
Run, my dear, from any one that may not strengthen
Your precious budding wings.
Run like hell, my dear, from any one prospective
To put a sharp knife into the sacred, tender vision
of your beautiful heart.
We have a duty to befriend those aspects of obedience
That stand outside of our house and shout to our reason,

"O please, O please, come out to play."
For we have not come here to take prisoners
Or to confine our wondrous spirits,
But to experience ever and ever more deeply
Our divine courage, freedom, and Light!

~Hafiz [4]

Put another way, although society, religion, and schools are rife with endless rules, life itself as Hafiz proclaims has "only one rule." Again, Hafiz expresses and emphasizes the "fun" that reflects the central experience of daily life at The Well School as if he were somehow present.

Only One Rule

The sky is suspended blue ocean,
The stars are the fish that swim.
The planets are white whales I sometimes hitch a ride on.
The sun and all light have forever fused themselves into my
Heart and upon my skin.
There is only one rule in the Wild Playground,
Every sign Hafiz has ever seen reads the same.
They all say,
Have fun, my dear, my dear have fun,
In the Beloved's divine Game,
O, the Beloved's Wondrous Game

~Hafiz 4

What is true of poetry's ability to approximate the ineffable ground of existence is true of the other arts as well. The Well School was based on a shared understanding of what empowers children to express themselves freely in the creative arts (in music, dance, drawing, painting, creative writing, theater, sculpture, batik, calligraphy, print making, mosaics, etc.) Many students first experienced success in one or several art forms.

Students' confidence in the arts led them to develop a unique, individual voice. It often led to academic success as well. Trust in themselves allowed them to learn how to create fruitful relationships, to take responsibility for keeping their school campus orderly, clean at the end of each day so that we were prepared for the next wonderful day. What permitted the students to access their inner wisdom and intuition, what empowered them and facilitated their genius, brilliance, and creativity, was initially that their teachers viewed them as unlimited. Over time, most students came to respect themselves, their peers, their parents, and their teachers.

A poem I wrote expresses this:

Inner Self

The violet, luminescent cauldron of creativity
harbors the primordial soup, the source of everything.
What are its ingredients, you ask?
Silence; Stillness; Peace; Harmony!
Unconditional Love; Sacred Sexuality;
The boon of Freedom to express Beauty;
effervescent Joy; ceaseless daring;

the pristine state of Original Innocence;
Mystery without end; Divine Grace!
The variegated, multitudinous tinctures of Truth;
promiscuous Appreciation of all that is; Sincerity;
an audacious, presumptuous Attitude;
seductive Symphony and simple Song!
Clear, focused, passion and drive!
What would you like to add to this luscious mixture
to make it even more sweet, more palliative,
more therapeutic, more exhilarating?

~Jay Garland [5]

Naked Education connects children to their essential, original nature, their inner, creative Being. Naked Education is an extension of life principles and the spiritual principles that underlie life. It supports Being (the original state of who we are, in touch with inner wisdom, inner knowing, what we were before we were born, the natural person before being conditioned by family, society, and culture), as well as Becoming. Naked Education therefore evolves from the inside out.

Our original, eternal, Divine spark can be forgotten and denied, but it is never lost. At some stage in our development, in this life or in a future one, we will remember our essential Self and consciously re-connect with our essence. This is the constant teaching of mystics through the ages. It is the basis of what is often called the "perennial philosophy" of ancient cultures around the world. This teaching is compatible with aboriginal and Native American teachings as well. It is central to Naked Education.

This intuition of our naked Self is naturally connected to the world in which we live and to the universe beyond. This wisdom manifests as unconditional love and peaceful equanimity. It leads naturally to seemingly effortless practical and artistic skills and permits us to live effectively and joyously in the outer world, expressing our true nature without fear or stress.

Abraham, a spokesman for "Vortex of Attraction", views the inner wisdom of children likewise:

Relative to our children or any children with whom we would interact, our one dominant intention would be to give them a conscious understanding of how powerful and important and valuable and perfect they are. Every word that would come out of our mouths would be a word that would be offered with the desire to help this individual know that they are powerful. It would be a word of empowerment. 6

~excerpted from Abraham-Hicks workshop 6

The purpose of Naked Education is to awaken individual potential and essence. Naked Education facilitates this awareness of children as being extremely gifted. Hafiz again beautifully expresses the euphoria, abundance, and intimacy that was central to Naked Education at The Well School.

So Many Gifts

There are so many gifts Still unopened from your birthday,
There are so many hand-crafted presents
That have been sent to you by God.
The Beloved does not mind repeating, "Everything I have is also yours."
Please forgive Hafiz and the Friend
If we break into sweet laughter
When your heart complains of being thirsty.
When ages ago
Every cell in your soul Capsized forever Into this infinite golden sea.
Indeed, A lover's pain is like holding one's breath
Too long In the middle of a vital performance,
In the middle of one of Creation's favorite Songs.
Indeed, a lover's pain is this sleeping,
This sleeping,
When God just rolled over and gave you
Such a big good-morning kiss!
There are so many gifts, my dear,
Still unopened from your birthday.

~Hafiz 4

Naked Education is but one form of authentic education. Authentic education, whatever its form, derives from spiritual principles and is based on a vision of individuals as fundamentally Spirit, as potential, ready to express and blossom. There have been other forms of authentic education, and there will be many more as we remember more vividly our source and our connection to our creator. Ernest Homes, an American New Thought thinker of the early and mid-twentieth century saw people in similar terms.

The following quote is from his book, *Creative Mind and Success*:

> *You are a center of divine attraction and the power within is going out and drawing back all that you need.*

~Ernest Holmes, *Creative Mind and Success* [7]

We must remember that spirituality is not religion. Rather it is the mystical experience of being connected with all that is. In the realm of emotion, it is experienced as unconditional love. It is not to be found in a mental vault of ideas, but in following what one intuitively and inwardly knows as truth.

The Well School was unique in many ways from its inception in 1967 to 2001, when Toni and Jay retired. Here are some of its most powerful structural innovations to education:

Going Home. Returning to our original nature reminds people of whom they have always been. The Well School was designed to empower children to remember their original self. Everything we did came from this central mission. We pushed the limits — we offered the children tremendous authority, matched only by enormous responsibility.

Class Meetings. We implemented an unparalleled environment for communication that we called "Class Meeting". Students in grades 1 through 4 met with nearly all their teachers. All parents were invited to attend as well and many did. Grades 5 through 8 did the same. Usually the Meeting was held weekly for two hours or as long at it took to resolve issues and conflicts, and to have presentations, demonstrations, or short performances.

Anyone attending Meeting could bring up any subject or any issue, praise or confront anyone present. The rules were simple: talk directly to and look at the person you wish to address; don't interrupt until someone has completed what they want to say; speak in a civil tone of voice. No whining! No victims! Take responsibility!

Besides the regular weekly Class Meeting, special meetings might be called by anyone who had a need to talk about something specific. This practice in communication skills made many of our students extremely articulate and well versed in communicating openly and honestly with adults and peers.

Parents as Teachers. Almost all the teachers in the school were parents. It was ideal to have parents who loved the children and taught only what they loved. We chose to be a state-approved school rather than a state-certified school because it allowed us to create our own curriculum and hire parents whose training had been in other fields: professionals (nurses, architects, lawyers, college professors, mathematicians), scientists (geologists, biologists, chemists), artists (painters, print makers, potters, paper makers, model makers, novelists, poets, playwrights, musicians), politicians, athletes, directors of music or drama, specialists in outdoor living, environmentalists, builders and carpenters, etc.

Joy in Learning. Less than half our school day addressed academic subjects. The majority of our school day was devoted to the Arts (Music, Dance, Drawing, Painting, Drama, Print Making, Ceramics, Mosaics, Silk Screen Printing, Book Making, Collage); Crafts (Sewing, Cooking, Baking, Knitting, Lamp Making, Flute Making, Model Making); Outdoor Activities (Birding, Plant Identification, Mountain Climbing, Biking, Exploring, Geology Field Trips); Sports (Hockey, Figure Skating, Soccer, Basketball, Eskimo Baseball); Martial Arts; Silent and Guided Meditation; and Yoga.

Although academic classes took up less than half a day, ironically our kids were far advanced in academics. Many were in the top five percentile of *all* the standardized tests they took.

Egalitarian Living. Although teachers had more responsibility than students, teachers saw students as their equals. They viewed kids as fully capable of spiritual, as well as mental and emotional growth. In fact, there were always students who surpassed their teacher or teachers in their ability to learn, to see life with greater perspective. Jay's Latin students sometimes surpassed him in knowledge of Latin. They could learn faster and feel comfortable with the language more readily. And while Jay found it difficult to memorize fully any play part, he asked his student to learn dozens, or hundreds of lines and gave out leading parts in excess of 500 lines that the actors learned and sometimes delivered flawlessly!

For a teacher to realize and acknowledge that many of his students surpassed him in so many ways made it easier for all students to see their own potential. After all, children are not miniature adults – they have the capacity to achieve things that adults cannot even dream of. They know they can help create a better world. Most adults have given up on that project. Before graduating in 8th grade, many of his charges had achieved what Jay had achieved by his college graduation.

Project Month. Project-based education, that is, learning by doing projects was part of a regular day. But, each year, the upper school (grades 5 through 8) finished their year with a month devoted to a multitude of specific projects, many taught by parents or friends of the school. Students for the most part chose the projects that interested them. Their creative energy and the joyful participation knew no bounds. See Chapter 4: The Role of "Project Month" in Book 3 of this series for a list of projects and their descriptions.

Love and Community. Putting into practice the ideal of unconditional love was our obsession. The natural, innocent expression of unconditional love means that touching and hugging and holding must be treasured in schools. For it is in an environment of habitual giving and receiving of love that children thrive. It is in an unconditioned loving atmosphere that kids surrender to their natural curiosity, surrender to a love of learning. When we realize that the purpose of life is to celebrate what we create together, we are united in joy. When we live that celebration daily, we have community. There is no genuine community without unconditional love.

Community is the living expression of love. It requires surrendering our right to be separate, our right to live in isolation physically and psychically. It requires of everyone that we relinquish our judgment of self and others, and see instead the goodness that dwells in all. We demonstrated the process of inclusion over decades. It was the cornerstone of our school community.

Metaphysical Background of Naked Education Philosophy

What is the philosophy that informs Naked Education?

Although I am and have been foremost a teacher, in many ways I also have the consciousness of a mystic. I am a person who seeks by contemplation and self-surrender to obtain unity with or absorption into the absolute; I am one who believes that the spiritual apprehension of truth and love lies beyond intellect, as artistic expression dwells beyond analytical thinking.

Mystics know that the invisible, subjective world precedes and creates the objective, visible world. This is because mystics have superseded the conscious mind and incorporated the knowledge of the unconscious mind. Although this idea has been accepted by the field of quantum physics, most scientists in our society still do not accept it. It is nevertheless a viewpoint that supports the unlimited creative nature of our Being and our vitality.

Mystics throughout the ages include the Gnostics, those searchers who derive inspiration from ancient sacred texts. The intuitive and knowledgeable aboriginal peoples, ancient mystics like Lao Tzu, philosophers like Plato, intuitive thinkers like Carl Jung and his modern day successor, James Hillman, have all known the basic Law of Consciousness.

Today, the fact that most people identify with the conditioned beliefs of their conscious mind and have no direct access to their unconscious mind, means they are totally ignorant of its contents and its powerful influence over them. Conscious humankind is so limited by its distorted "knowledge" and its conditioned opinions and judgments about who and what is "good and evil," "acceptable and deplorable," "fair and unfair", "insufferable and obnoxious," that they are unable to see the nature of what is, and blinded as well to what they most deeply desire.

Our personal unconscious is filled with what ego rejected as "forbidden" and "unthinkable." It houses so many negative and limiting beliefs about ourselves and others, about what is impossible and unviable, that it nullifies our deepest desires and precludes our getting what we truly want and desperately need.

I have opened this Pandora's box in myself through years of weekly sessions of muscle testing. Muscle testing is a way of determining unconscious beliefs by testing the strength or weakness of specific muscles when asked specific questions – strength indicates an affirmative answer, weakness a "no." Muscle testing, also known by its formal name, "applied kinesiology," can determine what blocks the easy fulfillment of personal desires, and helps address negative beliefs held by the unconscious about what frustrates my deepest longings. Fortunately reversing these negative beliefs through additional muscle testing is a simple, quick process.

Prayer is also capable of changing unconscious assumptions. Prayer ignores the outside world of sense perceptions and the external truths based on sensations. It focuses instead on connecting consciousness with inner Self in the present moment. One's faith in the process of directly anticipating a relationship with Spirit, waiting for the still, soft, inner voice to speak, short-circuits reason. A humble, unreasoned petition works wonders!

The common practice of prayer, petitioning for something or some desired condition, is ineffective and wrong-headed. Prayer is not about asking some exterior god for what one wants, whether it be things or conditions. Effective prayer invokes rapport between the subconscious and conscious mind within us. Prayer is about listening to one's inner Being, being in the receptive mode. When that connection is established through listening, then "miracles" become possible. Faith in prayer short-circuits what is "reasonable and possible" to attain what is otherwise truly "spontaneous and impossible."

The conscious mind reasons from what it observes from experience and what it absorbs from education and then forms premises based on its observations and what it is taught. The subconscious automatically accepts the premises of consciousness and unfolds or objectifies them.

The hypnotic state, or controlled reverie, also short-circuits the rational process because it embodies unconscious objectivity. The control of the subjective mind through mental suggestion bypasses reason.

The conscious generates ideas and impresses these ideas on the subconscious; the subconscious receives ideas and gives form and expression to them. According to this law – first making a premise and then impressing it on the subconscious – all things evolve out of consciousness. Most of us have it backwards: we ascribe our feelings to particular events that randomly occur in the exterior environment, thereby denying that conditions in the world, as we perceive them, accurately and automatically reflect our thinking and feeling.

When we surrender to and become aligned with our greater Self, we are defined anew; we assume a new identity, an identity of our choosing. The process that furthers this radical, sudden transformation of identity has been described by many authors: George Winslow Plummer's book published in 1939, *Consciously Creating Circumstances*; Neville Goddard's *The Five Lessons, Feeling is the Secret, The Law is the Promise, Awakened Imagination and The Neville Reader*; *The Law of Attraction* by Esther Hicks and Jerry Hicks (the teaching about how to create your own reality can also be found in recordings of innumerable workshops available from www.abraham-hicks.com); Adyashanti's *Falling into Grace, The Way of Liberation, and Shift into Freedom*; Paramahansa Yogananda's *Autobiography of a Yogi*, and *The Yoga of the Bhagavad Gita*. See also *Science of Mind* by Ernest Holmes and Joel Goldsmiths' *Practicing the Presence*, as well as *The Infinite Way*. These texts are all precursors to Naked Education.

> *All things when they are admitted, are made manifest by the light for everything that is made manifest is light.*
>
> ~*Holy Bible*, Ephesians 5:13 8

Naked Education teaches that consciousness is our only true Self. Consciousness manifests by a person consciously and consistently deciding to become his or her deepest nature. Although this consciousness is one, it manifests in many forms and levels of awareness. We can choose to be the arbiter of our fate through choosing more advanced self-concepts; changing identity determines a new world in which we live. Our mind is congruent with the image of all we believe and consent to as true about our self.

Until we choose to raise our consciousness, we cannot take this fast path to changing our world through changing ourselves. We all live according to how we have been programmed to believe by our family and our society. This original, low-level consciousness determines our life as we experience it. And since our consciousness is all that we think, desire and love, all that we think is true and consent to, our inner *transformation* depends on refreshing our mind with radically new ideas, that is *evolving*, becoming someone different from who we were before. We cannot upgrade the quality of our experience without first increasing our awareness of Self.

"Naked Education teaches that transformation first requires an intense desire to be transformed. That is, one must intend and want to be different before one can change himself or herself. You must first align your future dream with present fact. This is done by assuming the feeling of our desire fulfilled – that is by assuming you are already what you desire to be. By persisting in that assumption, by suspending doubt, one attains the ideal.

It is a common, yet delusional conviction that there are causes other than our consciousness that create our life as we experience it. The greatest ally of awareness is *imagination*.

> *I rest not from my great task*
> *To Open the eternal worlds, to open the immortal Eyes*
> *Of man inwards into the Worlds of Thought into Eternity*
> *Ever expanding in the Bosom of God, the human Imagination*
> >   ~William Blake, *Jerusalem; 5:18-20* [9]

> *I am enough of an artist to draw freely upon my imagination. Imagination is more important than knowledge. For knowledge is limited, whereas imagination embraces the entire world, stimulating progress, giving birth to evolution.*
> >   ~Albert Einstein [10]

> *The first power that meets us at the threshold of the soul's domain is the power of imagination.*
> >   ~Dr. Franz Hartmann [11]

The imagination, give it the least license, dives deeper and soars higher than Nature does.

~Henry David Thoreau, The Writings of Henry David Thoreau [12]

That which men suppose the imagination to be, and to do, is often frivolous enough and mischievous enough; but that which God meant it to be in the mental economy is not merely noble, but super eminent. It is the distinguishing element in all refinement. It is the secret and marrow of civilization. It is the very eye of faith. The soul without imagination is what an observatory would be without a telescope.

~Henry Ward Beecher, [14]

Naked Education assumes that transformation to higher reality requires suspending self-criticism and embracing *Imagination* as the means to escape sickness, slavery, and poverty. *Imagination*, aligned with one's deepest desires and wants, transforms. For one's oceanic desires come from Spirit, not ego. To dare to fulfill them through *Imagination*, to dare to experience them as a reality, transforms one's former identity in order to adopt a more conscious, evolved one. By making those desires conscious and *Imagining* them already real, feeling and dwelling in the immediacy of it all, alters one's identity, and transforms reality, both the inner vision and the outer experience.

But *refusing* the responsibility of personally incarnating an original, new view of reality kills what might be – dead in its tracks.

Rather than developing the imagination of its students, our traditional educational system regularly stifles imaginative thinking. This forces students to:

Memorize a number of text books which, all too soon, are disproved by later text books. Education is not accomplished by putting something into man; its purpose is to draw out of man the wisdom which is latent within him."

~Neville Goddard, *Your Faith is Your Fortune* [16]

Transformation is *not* part of the natural evolutionary process. Without a resolute, major personal decision to effect change, one loses momentum and slips back into the old, tired habit that dominates and controls one's mind and identity.

In my experience the willingness to die to your present self and create from sustained imagination the self you desire to be, creates greater awareness. Through focused imagination and intense feeling, change of identity requires a series of small successive deaths and reinventions of Self.

These "rebirths" are possible for anyone thoroughly dissatisfied with himself. Only one with a conscious, daily, determined desire to upgrade and expand one's identity, to be radically different from what one has repeatedly experienced as one's reliable nature, can be "reborn." The fact that this radical growth process was the living center of Naked Education at The Well School – that, one way or another it remained a focal point at single-class or multi-class Meetings, meant we regularly and habitually observed radical changes in each other.

Because we at The Well School weekly focused on and discussed these possibilities of transformation, it became the norm to see these capacities in each other and express openly what we observed. Mentioning the greatness we perceived in each other as a matter of course naturally led to a new group mentality: everyone who chose to could be transfigured. That was the reality we, as a group, aspired to. That was the reality each individual could accept and adopt as his or her own, or reject if he or she so wished. That "reality," that most powerful possibility, informs Naked Education. Purposeful, internal change is the heart of transformational education. The supreme test of imagination and the supreme goal of Naked Education is the forgiveness of sins that necessitates in the process, forgiveness of Self through the process of forgiving others.

Focusing on possibilities rather than complaining about the mundane, present, negative and "unfair" reality, opens the portal to the power of Naked Education. In all cases, however, the individual must be dedicated to increasing his awareness if it was to become hardened fact instead of just a possibility.

Six Perspectives on The Well School – Six Books on Naked Education

Even before we opened the doors to The Well School, it was clear to Toni and me that there was an unseen force at work, guiding us as we developed the school. It was as if a plan for a new school had already been fully developed, a plan beyond our comprehension, and we were only the custodians of this plan. We understood this to be true throughout our years of involvement as parents, teachers, and directors.

We were always at a loss to adequately describe this creation. Oddly, many parents trusted us implicitly from the start and needed no coherent explanation of what we would teach. Inexplicably, there were families that seemed to have made up their minds to enroll their children even before they met us or had a tour of the campus.

When we developed a brochure explaining the school to prospective Well School parents, it was obvious that the true nature of the school could not be put into words or pictures. Parents told us that when they described The Well School to friends or relatives, others could not understand what they were talking about. It lay beyond their experience. One had to visit The Well, one had to experience it many times to know what it was about.

It wasn't until we retired that we were able to understand and write cogently about our experience at The Well. Only then did we have the perspective to appreciate the scope of our efforts during our thirty-four, very busy years. Yet, rather than having in our possession a series of images that fit together to make up a complete picture, we were left with individual snapshots. Each snapshot offered us a chance to view The Well from a unique perspective.

There are six perspectives that we flesh out in our writing, corresponding to the six books of the Naked Education series. The sequence may not be important from a reader's point of view as each stands independently on its own. Considered together, these perspectives form a comprehensive picture of The Well, based on our experience.

Be forewarned, the introduction to "Naked Education" appears in all the six books of this series! This is done by design because this initial assessment is so important and so unique, it must be repeated over time to totally sink into consciousness. This introduction is the very root and heart of Naked Education. From experience, I have found that to become familiar with a new paradigm requires repeated reading of its basic tenets. Although one can begin to grasp its basic principles, little of significance penetrates and soaks in at first. I have to reread material that challenges my basic assumptions about life multiple times before I am able to be truly receptive to it so that it penetrates my worldview. Books I treasure most I have reread every few years and still new meanings emerge that make me wonder how particular viewpoints evaded my scrutiny in earlier readings. Often it seems like I have never before read certain passages even when I have already marked them with a pen as significant.

The reader may grasp the full importance of a message faster then I can. Yet I believe there is little danger in rereading seminal ideas over and over again.

Afterword Note:

For the past three decades I have collected quotes from many of my favorite authors and from many books that are collections of famous quotations, several of which identified the author of the quotation but not the source books from which they were taken.

Therefore the Notes at the end of each book sometimes contain the Author, Title, Publisher, Place of Publication, and Date of Publication. For many Endnotes, however, the full information was not available; this is reflected in Notes that contain only the author, or just the author and title, but not full citations.

ADDITIONAL NOTE:

If any of the readers of the series wish to communicate with Jay or Toni, or both, either to suggest corrections to the text, or to comment in any way about any of the books in the series, to make suggestions, to ask questions, or to start a new conversation, our e-mail addresses is jay@jtgarland.com or toni@jtgarland.com or authors@jtgarland.com. Or read our blog at: http://newearthinstitute.blogspot.com/2010/03/jay-and-toni-garland-bio.html. If anyone would like assistance in starting a school, the authors will do what they can to assist, including traveling to where a group of you live to meet with you and discuss the methods of Naked Education.

NOTES:

Chapter 1: Ideas from Book 1

In Book One of *Naked Education: Joyful Learning in a School Community*, we discussed the founding and development of the community of The Well School in Peterborough, New Hampshire, a school that taught day students in grades K–8 (sometimes K–9, sometimes K–12). This school was built on the paradigm of Inclusion, and on the community of teachers, students, and parents who practiced its principles.

This paradigm of Inclusion expresses a specific consciousness, a way of living together in community while honoring the following:

1. *The integrity and distinctive talents of each child*

2. *The need of each child to grow in awareness, to gain spiritual and intellectual independence*

3. *The need for regular self-expression: to develop a personal voice in dealing with relationships and an artistic "voice" in various art forms*

4. *The need to be given freedom according to one's ability to accept and discharge responsibility*

5. *The individual and the group search for Truth*

6. *The need to connect with the life force*

Such a community requires teachers who:

1. *Respect and treasure each child*

2. *Possess an active curiosity to gain knowledge about the inner Self and about the exterior world*

3. *Love what they are teaching*

4. *Are sensitive to goodness, truth, and beauty*

5. *Can laugh at themselves and relax*

It is also important to involve parents in the education of their children in one or both of the following:

1. *Teaching on a full – or part-time basis*

2. *Sharing some special knowledge, talent, or passion with members of the school community*

For us, the main purpose of education is to nourish the inner being of each individual by developing a community whose attitudes and ideas support emotional, intellectual and spiritual development.

The founders (who are also the authors of this book) saw the need for a new perspective in education, the need to base education on the *inner nature* and the *highest potential* of each child. Because we view the child as divine in essence – potentially capable of turning to the inner Self for guidance, instruction, and wisdom – our educational focus was on recognizing and facilitating the expression of each child's particular genius. We were dedicated, therefore, to supporting as many avenues as possible in which human intelligence and talents could be expressed.

We see the student not as one who must adapt to the limitations and prejudices of his society, but as one whose primary need is to discover his own potential as both an individual and as a compassionate human being, as well as the ability to see the greatness in those around him, including his peers, his teachers, and his parents. Since we saw genius as plural, as multiple, or as multi-faceted, our goal was to assist each child in expressing a host of his innate, hidden qualities: specific sensibilities, intelligences, and talents that set him apart from others.

Our chief concern as teachers was the state of our own consciousness, for our experience taught us that a teacher's awareness determines the level of consciousness in the classroom. A teacher's consciousness determines her expectations and her agenda. Her awareness determines the appropriateness of every activity and the response to every behavior. An open and aware teacher will recognize and reflect back the spiritual qualities of her students. When she creates an environment of order and safety, the inner life of her students can blossom.

Such a teacher, therefore, is not primarily concerned with imparting knowledge about the outer world, that is, with teaching a specific curriculum. To do so would only separate the child from its own Being. Instead, her goal is to engage the inner Being of her students, as well as their outer nature, in the process of learning. Such a teacher assumes that her students possess a powerful inner Being; she understands that she is dealing with Beings of infinite worth. She addresses first the inner needs of the child to:

1. *Express his thoughts, feelings, and intimations*

2. *Be part of a greater whole without sacrificing his individual perspective*

3. *Know his strengths and confront his weaknesses; to accept responsibility without blaming or faulting others*

4. *Respect and honor self and others*

5. *Live as brothers and sisters with his peers*

6. *Support each other in their striving*

7. *Do his or her best*

8. *Work out problems; to forgive self and others; to work and play together*

9. *Honor truth; to grow in consciousness; to learn from and be guided by experience*

10. *Communicate clearly with others; to examine one's assumptions of what others think or want*

11. *Accept ever more responsibility for himself*

A teacher who knows her students from a spiritual perspective, knows what materials to bring into her lessons to further both their spiritual and intellectual development. If she is given the authority to revise her curriculum according to the needs of her students and herself, she can call upon what feeds her as an individual to supplement her curriculum so that her own inner Being is nourished in the process of nourishing her students. What she loves enlivens her teaching because she can teach directly from her Soul. When her teaching provides for the flow of life energy for herself and her students, all are nourished, all prosper, all grow together, all unite in positive energy.

If neither the teacher nor the students find nourishment and joy in the educational process, Naked Education ceases. All activity becomes anathema to Spirit. Joyless, repetitive education dulls students and exhausts teachers; all simply survive in isolation.

We know that teachers and students who lack life and a natural responsiveness to each other nevertheless adapt and carry on; however, they perform only the routines. School becomes a factory of mechanical procedures, form without substance, a pretense of education, but a deadly game in which all involved become as the walking dead.

The Well School focused on the importance of the development of consciousness. It was our greatest priority because we understood that elevated consciousness furthers:

1. *Ability to succeed at all levels*

2. *Living in harmony with humankind*

3. *Seeing the goodness in and feeling compassion for others*

4. *The Power to attract peace and joy into one's life*

5. *The sense of abundance and well-being*

6. *Partnership with nature and the creative universe*

If our consciousness includes the knowledge that our joy, our serenity, and our ability to love Self and others depends on our awareness, and not on what others do to us or for us, life becomes a wonderful challenge, and solutions to problems are relatively simple.

Consciousness can be pictured as a vertical hierarchy. At the top are joyful activity, flexibility, service, and devotion. At the bottom lie selfishness, fear, and arrogance. And between the extremes are the thousands of steps, or levels, or rungs on the ladder to total awareness. Each step gained in the ascent confers to an individual more inner power and authority over Self and the environment; each step of descent marks the forfeiture of one's power in order to attain a transient goal.

Of course, the system of the industrialized world has its own ladder. At the top is accumulated wealth, power over others, and ego aggrandizement. Poverty, subservience, and self-loathing lie at the bottom. This system is based on the belief that in the exterior world of appearances, popularity, and control of others is the measure of man. Rising near the top never satisfies, however, because there is always the need to acquire more, and there is always the fear of falling. Even at the ladder's heights, the soft voice of Spirit still speaks of a higher perspective and of richer possibilities. This creates in most the need to block out the voice, stay busy, keep thinking, or become addicted to pleasures that consume one's consciousness.

Although our school was spiritually based, we taught no religious dogma, nor were we affiliated with any religious institution. Instead, we provided the flexibility for all who wished to follow their own inner authority. Classes within the school often read portions of sacred texts from cultures around the world. And throughout the school, we informally taught simple spiritual principles: inclusion, kindness, honesty, and honoring Self, among others. Rather than subscribe to mental constructs of sin and evil, we encouraged all to become more conscious of themselves.

We provided an extended weekly forum, in the round, for students and teachers to discuss whatever they wished. We required all to express themselves in a civil tone of voice, but we encouraged full expression. There were no taboo subjects, for we trusted in the process of openness, the expression of spoken feelings and ideas, as well as expression through writing, music, art, dance, and theater.

We provided a similar forum in Family Conferences, which included parents, teachers, and students. Here, again, everything was up for discussion, for criticism or praise, for investigation, in order to determine in the end what was best for the child and for the group as a whole.

Because we believe that Naked Education requires the genuine expression of all, we welcomed candor. Expanding consciousness demands ever more individual expression, both positive and negative. When expression is blocked, the flow of life force is stifled, impeded.

To confront a person with his own shadow is to show him his own light.

~Carl Jung [1]

It is a mark of our civilization that all people carry within a shadow self. This shadow self is the repressed part of our nature, the part of ourselves we cannot accept, the part we hide from our ego and the world.

But as Carl Jung pointed out, the shadow self holds the key to tremendous untapped power and new awareness. But only when the shadow can emerge and receive acknowledgment can it become integrated with the conscious self and so unleash its potential. Our consciousness, and hence our power, is enlarged each time we take responsibility for our hidden nature, each time we wake up and free ourselves from the unconscious aspects of our Being that have been tied to emotions of shame, guilt, and fear.

There is nothing either good or bad but thinking makes it so.

~Shakespeare [2]

A person who acknowledges his great gifts, as well as his weaknesses and superficialities, can evolve spiritually. So The Well School encouraged all to see and express both the greatness and the weakness in self, and to move on into greater consciousness. To fail to do this is to be stuck in a life of hypocrisy, hiding one's "badness" while trying to convince others of one's "goodness." One-upmanship, as a life strategy, delays consciousness; it is exhausting and self-defeating.

He who falls in love with himself will have no rivals.

~Anonymous

We wanted all of our students to fulfill their highest potential and become spiritual warriors who think and decide for themselves. We wanted them to trust their own inner guidance and to test the truth of what authorities proclaimed.

The riches that are in the heart cannot be stolen.

~Russian Proverb

We wanted all to learn to live through their hearts so that they might become genuine human Beings connected with mankind.

All paths are the same: they lead nowhere. They are paths going through the bush, or into the bush. In my own life I could say I have traversed long, long paths but I am not anywhere. My benefactor's question has meaning now. Does this path have a heart? If it does, the path is good; if it doesn't, it is of no use. Both paths lead nowhere; but one has a heart, the other doesn't. One makes for a joyful journey; as long as you follow it, you are one with it. The other will make you curse your life. One makes you strong; the other weakens you.

~Carlos Castaneda, *The Teachings of Don Juan* [3]

My own educational experience had convinced me that following traditional thinking meant personal death. In grades 1-12, my public schools asked nothing of my inner Being which ached to express itself. The schools cared only about my performance; otherwise, I was invisible.

As a student at Harvard College, I was suffocated by the materialistic thinking of my teachers, which always seemed disconnected to practical life, to real life.

At first I was thrilled to be immersed in theoretical thinking about a wide variety of topics. I completely bought into the idea that I was my thoughts, that my thinking defined me. I could alter myself by changing my thoughts. After a while my thought life became the only life I knew. I believed I could think my way into and out of realities, could solve problems simply by analyzing them. I accepted that my worth depended on my ability to make a clever point, to see from a unique angle.

At last I realized I was not only disoriented, but I was lost. I had given away one frame of reference for another, and then another. I was grasping at straws. The intellectual game had swallowed me. I became strongly oppressed by my environment, my acquaintances, my classes, my teachers. I ceased to function in any meaningful way. I was, as I see now, a fearful ego out of touch with my living Being. I had lost my center of gravity and didn't know how to re-orient myself.

I turned within to find myself. I looked at my situation. I was horrified by the consequences of an unbalanced intellectual environment: the morbidity, the smugness, the arrogance of people disconnected from life Spirit. This arrogance was not confined to the undergraduate level. I used to visit the law school cafeteria for their tasty food and talked to many depressed and suicidal law students who were intelligent, but suffocating in the lifeless, stifling atmosphere of the institution.

You must understand the whole of life, not just one little part of it. That is why you must read, that is why you must look at the skies, that is why you must sing, and dance, and write poems, and suffer, and understand, for all that is life.

~J. Krishnamurti, *Think On These Things* 4

My ego could no longer manage. I was swamped by the endless theorizing. I collapsed from exhaustion, spent weeks in the Harvard infirmary with an undiagnosed ailment, and began to read literature from the East.

I was discharged after medical tests failed to discover a disease. I survived the suffocating college atmosphere by involuntarily leaving my body for long periods of time. My center of consciousness seemed to float outside my body, approximately a foot behind my left shoulder blade. When out of body, I felt safe but without a solid center of gravity. Whether in or out of my body, I was actively searching for a meaningful identity.

In the spring of my freshman year, I was drawn to another student as if by a fateful force. In his presence I lost my shyness and reticence. We developed our own life style and schedule out of sync with the college schedule. We talked and played and wrote by night and slept through all our classes.

In my sophomore year, I married my childhood sweetheart, Toni, and left the deadly dormitory life for another world where I somehow discovered a new orientation. I was blissful and on firm ground.

As a college senior I wrote for my amusement, or more accurately I felt compelled to write a prospectus for an anti-school, one designed primarily to nourish the heart and Spirit, to celebrate the inner life force. This school would later become The Well School.

The Well School was designed to create enthusiasm and energy among the students, while at the same time instilling strong habits of discipline, concentration, and cooperation. The school's activities primarily engaged the heart and Spirit, and served as outlets for individual energy and expression.

Book 1: Joyful Learning in a School Community describes the history of how our school was formed, how it was named The Well School, and how Meetings, Parent Conferences, and general school ideals served to support the principle of Inclusion.

NOTES:

NOTES:

Chapter 2: The Challenge of Consciousness in Education

Something we were withholding made us weak until we found it was ourselves.

~Robert Frost [1]

Our business is to wake up. We have to find ways in which to detect the whole of reality in the one illusory part which our self-centered consciousness permits us to see. We must not live thoughtlessly, taking our illusion for the complete reality, but at the same time we must not live too thoughtfully in the sense of trying to escape from the dream state. We must be continuously on our watch for ways in which we may enlarge our consciousness.

~Aldous Huxley [2]

In my mind, schools either wake up students to their inner genius, their inner life force, their ability to follow their own star, their multiple talents, and their life possibilities, or schools help create a hypnotic spell that puts students into a waking sleep in which their consciousness remains isolated from their very Being. Naked Education, for me, leads to self-discovery, self-expression, self-realization. Repressive education demands that students adapt to a lifeless, inhuman system.

People say that what we're all seeking is a meaning for life. I don't think that's what we're really seeking. I think that what we're really seeking is an experience of being alive, so that our life experiences on the purely physical plane will have resonances with our innermost Being and reality, so that we can actually feel the rapture of being alive.

~Joseph Campbell, *The Power of Myth* [3]

Walk into any school. Are you not capable, after a few minutes' observation, of telling if the students are alive, expressive, thrilled to be there? Can you discern if the system shuts down the individuals, or if the students are free to express their individuality?

Another crucial question for me is: Do the students have permission to express affection for their fellow students or teachers, and does the teacher demonstrate her love for the children, or is the demonstration of natural affection, of love for each other, taboo? Where love abides, life flourishes; where love is stifled, a campaign of death reigns.

> *There is a land of the living and a land of the dead, and the bridge is love, the only survival, the only meaning.*
>
> ~Thornton Wilder [4]

Does the teacher provoke the students to think, does she lead the students to new realizations? Does she awaken them?

> *If the personal relationship of the child to the teacher is a good one, it matters very little whether the method of teaching is the most up-to-date. Success does not depend on the method, any more than it is the exclusive aim of school life to stuff the children's heads with knowledge, but rather to make them real men and women. We need not concern ourselves so much with the amount of specific information a child takes away with him from school; the thing of vital importance is that the school should succeed in freeing the young man from unconscious identity with his family, and should make him properly conscious of himself. Without this consciousness he will never know what he really wants, but will always remain dependent and imitative, with the feeling of being misunderstood and suppressed.*
>
> ~Jung, *Development of Personality* [5]

Can you feel a dynamic energy in the classroom? Are you aware of a living presence?

> *What is really important in education is not that the child learns this or that, but that the mind is matured, that energy is aroused.*
>
> ~Sören Kierkegaard, *Either/Or* [6]

Our concerns about the presence of life and energy and an atmosphere of love, the recognition of the inner life of a student and the recognition of his need to express himself, are all focused on the presence or absence of consciousness in a classroom. Yes, many of us have experienced an education devoid of consciousness, devoid of life, devoid of personal meaning. But the world is fast awakening to evidence that increased consciousness not only combats many of the evils of modern society – stress, illness, depression, hopelessness, isolation – but also allows individuals to discover meaning, to regulate the direction of their lives, and to blossom as creative personalities and as superior, inquisitive students. Greater consciousness inevitably connects us with our inner Being, reveals our true nature, and allows us to experience beauty and purpose as an integrated, whole human Being.

A statue lies hidden in a block of marble, and the statuary only clears away the superfluous matter and removes the rubbish. The figure is in the stone: the sculptor only finds it.

A highly conscious individual intuitively knows many things from *within* without instruction. She is naturally compassionate, moral, and truthful, for she has seen through her false mask and contacted her inner authenticity.

You are always your own best guru, your own best teacher. The answers are always inside you.

~Sai Baba [7]

In an atmosphere of love, the heart is awakened, opened, expanded so that we become reconnected to the riches of the mythic world, so that we know things intuitively and directly, so that we communicate from our inner Being. When the heart is alive and active, we have a personal relationship with others. A personal education is authentic because it is centered in the active heart, not on the abstractions and generalizations of the head.

I am against revolutions because they always involve a return to the status quo. I am against the status quo both before and after revolutions. I don't want to wear a black shirt or a red shirt. I want to wear the shirt that suits my taste. And I don't want to salute like an automaton either. I prefer to shake hands when I meet someone I like. The fact is, to put it simply, I am positively against all this crap which is carried on first in the name of this thing, then in the name of that. I believe only what is active, immediate, and personal.

~Henry Miller [8]

In Naked Education, it is the heart that discriminates more than the mind. The heart directly apprehends beauty and truth. Naked Education's curriculum is built not around endless factual information, but around beauty and truth.

> *There is a field where all wonderful perfections of microscope and telescope fail. All exquisite niceties of weights and measures as well as that which is behind them, the keen and driving power of the mind. No facts, however indubitably detected, no effort of reason, however magnificently maintained, can prove that Bach's music is beautiful.*

> ~Edith Hamilton [9]

The heart intuits the connection we have with others, with all sentient beings, with every wonder of the universe because it feels awe and wonder and the mystery of love. The compassion of the heart embraces all the world.

> *I have heard of reasons manifold*
> *Why Love must needs be blind,*
> *But his the best of all I hold –*
> *His eyes are in my mind.*
> *What outward form and features are*
> *He guesseth but in part.*
> *But what within is good and fair*
> *He seeth with the heart.*

> ~Samuel Coleridge [10]

My Heart Leaps Up

> *My heart leaps up when I behold*
> *A rainbow in the sky:*
> *So was it when my life began;*
> *So is it now I am a man;*
> *So be it when I shall grow old,*
> *Or let me die!*
> *The Child is father of the Man;*
> *And I could wish my days to be*
> *Bound each to each in natural piety.*

> ~William Wordsworth [11]

Love is the bridge from death to life, from despair to joy, from isolation to re-connection. Love re-introduces us to our inner compassion, to our inner wisdom. If schools teach life instead of death, they honor the inner beauty and infinite worth of every child, and speak directly to each child's heart and inner Being, and thus consciously address the Divine within. If schools teach life, instead of death, they address each child as the consciousness that dwells within, and so recognize and enliven the consciousness of each Being.

Man is that part of reality in which and through which the cosmic process has become conscious and has begun to comprehend itself. His supreme task is to increase that conscious comprehension and to apply it as fully as possible to guide the course of events. In other words, his role is to discover his destiny as agent of the evolutionary process, in order to fulfill it more adequately.

~Julian Huxley, *Religion Without Revelation* [12]

When education is devoted to nourishing life and awakening the treasure of inner life, to fostering individual consciousness at every turn, it must serve to connect each student with his own Being, and with the mythology of earlier ages, which symbolically teaches him or her about inner Self and about positive and destructive relationships. Naked Education helps students express inner life in a variety of creative endeavors: writing, art, music, dance, theater, and storytelling. It exposes students to the authentic, living expression of others: including the world's great art and literature.

In my hunt for the secret of life, I started my research in histology. Unsatisfied by the information that cellular morphology could give me about life, I turned to physiology. Finding physiology too complex I took up pharmacology. Still finding the situation too complicated I turned to bacteriology. But bacteria were even too complex, so I descended to the molecular level, studying chemistry and physical chemistry. After twenty years' work, I was led to conclude that to understand life we have to descend to the electronic level, and to the world of wave mechanics. But electrons are just electrons, and have no life at all. Evidently on the way I lost life; it had run out between my fingers.

~Albert Szent-Gyorgyi, *Personal Reflections* [13]

You may recognize that in almost every field of human endeavor, the degree of consciousness of an individual determines the quality of his or her life, and consequently, his or her work. It is not money or educational degrees or political or economic pull that guarantees the quality of architecture, artistic expression, moral decisions, medical care, or political decisions; nor do those materialistic factors determine the quality of media information, neighborhood cooperation, police behavior, or education. It is the level of consciousness of the individuals involved that counts, which is reflected in the conditions of the life it creates.

As an individual moves beyond wanting to look good and be well liked, to a larger awareness of cooperation and compassion, of concern for the good of all, his effect on everybody and everything he touches changes. He who moves beyond concerns for the self, blesses and sustains whatever he touches.

We are shaped and fashioned by what we love.

~Johann Wolfgang von Goethe [14]

Consciousness is the key to life, significantly affecting both everyday experiences and crucial decisions. Can we not now realize that when a person is negatively entrapped by self-centered ego concerns, she spreads her toxicity wherever she goes? But she who becomes a full human being spreads light wherever life may lead. Advanced consciousness is a power that spreads Love to advance good will on earth.

Without a major change in human consciousness, man's inhumanity to man, woman, child, and our environment – which is simply a reflection of the ego-driven mind obsessed with its perceived, but illusory, fears – will never cease. Our ancient collective reality, sustained by our daily reactions of egoic fear, keeps us unconscious, violent, laden with accumulated negativity, painfully separated from and opposed to our true Self and the outer world.

Since everything is but an apparition
Perfect in being what it is,
Having nothing to do with good or bad,
Acceptance or rejection,
One may well burst out in laughter.

~Longchenpa [15]

Inhumanity, I have learned, is caused when we are out of touch with our inner Being. It is the common trademark of the ego, which acts out of illusory fear. Although its forms differ, every ego's interest is the same. When it falsely identifies with a distortion of the truth of its own Being, it defines itself as a separate, vulnerable body subject to death. It identifies with its name, its unconscious fearful images and thoughts, its perceived reputation, and thereby becomes an isolated refugee in a dangerous world. Ego depends on its own cleverness to survive each day. Its primary strategy is to identify with things, roles, places, bodies, and conditions it judges "good" for its benefit, and to resist everything it deems "bad." It thus becomes a victim of both good and bad circumstances. Its "happiness" depends on having the "good;" its frustration, its sense of impotency, its misery, its blame, its anger or jealousy or rage or sadness, its boredom, or its deprivation of what it craves, depends on feeling victimized by the "bad." Ego unconsciously and fallaciously believes that it can magically drive away the "bad" and promulgate the "good."

Its defensiveness, its resistance to all things or conditions it has pronounced "bad," creates conflict and, step by step, further separates the ego from the unconscious life force, from all that exists, and from the present moment. The ego cannot perceive the wonder and power of what is now because it is controlled obsessively and ruthlessly by past regrets and future hopes. Its imagination of the past and future, therefore, creates a self-centered drama that runs its life; ego suffers each time it resists what is. Since the ego's consciousness is extremely limited, it cannot even question its basic assumptions, and will fight to the death to preserve its pathetic identity while it psychically pollutes its environment.

Oh, you who are trying to learn the marvel of Love through the copy book of reason, I'm very much afraid that you will never really see the point.

~Hafiz of Shiraz [16]

When we have attained higher consciousness, even temporarily, we do not resist life, but accept what is. At that point, our emotional and mental state does not depend on things being a certain way, so we remain fully empowered, and escape the debilitating negativity of resistance; then we are open to deal with what meets us in our present moment.

Remember that your perception of the world is only a reflection of your state of consciousness. You are not separate from it, and there is no objective world out there. Every moment your consciousness creates the particular, individual world that you inhabit. One of the greatest insights that has come out of modern physics is the unity between the observer and the observed: the person conducting an experiment – the observing consciousness – cannot be separated from the observed phenomena. A different way of looking causes the observed phenomena to behave differently!

With an increased awareness, we can remain free agents, able to make a conscious, positive choice about our present reality. We remain connected and in tune with the life force. With no resistance, no blame, no negativity, we are not controlled by unconscious forces; we can be loving and non-reactive. We can make decisions from a peaceful state of being. We can have straightforward, positive relationships with others that are, for the most part, free of drama. We can feel and be compassionate, sympathizing with the vulnerability of others who, out of fear, identify with the body that dies. We can also support the true, immortal being that lives within the living, inner body.

The realization of this deathless dimension, your true nature, is the other side of compassion. On the deep feeling level, you now recognize not only your own immortality but through your own that of every other living creature as well. On the level of form, you share mortality and the precariousness of existence. On the level of Being, you share eternal, radiant life.

~Eckhart Tolle, *The Power of Now* [17]

Every being is a focal point of consciousness, and every such focal point creates its own world, although all those worlds are interconnected. ... Highly conscious beings who are aware of their connectedness with the Source and with each other would inhabit a world that to you would appear as a heavenly realm – and yet all worlds are ultimately one.

~Eckhart Tolle, *The Power of Now* [17]

Does it not naturally follow that only an education that significantly raises consciousness can be called "Naked Education," whether it occurs within a family, a small community school, or a large city establishment? This is the conclusion Toni and I reached before founding The Well School, while we were teaching the Inuit children in Alaska. For us, the purpose of conscious education was revealed in the open and generous attitude and actions of the Inuit people there.

NAKED EDUCATION: Book 3: Activities that Expand Consciousness is a book about the tremendous potential benefits of conscious education and the potential harm of ignoring consciousness. In the field of education, Toni and I believe that the importance of raising consciousness trumps whatever type of factual knowledge one gains in school. Knowledge, as we all know, can be used to destroy as well as to build, to confuse and cheat as well as to clarify. Our use of knowledge depends on our general level of consciousness. And we believe that she who possesses an enlightened awareness will draw every good thing to herself and to others who are fortunate enough to come into her sphere of influence. The guiding principle here, the invisible yet powerfully directive force of consciousness, according to our degree of awareness, creates the visible and invisible conditions of our life.

It is all a question of perspective. As long as educators perceive a child as a limited survivor, as one lacking inner purpose and inner power, they will try to mold him according to society's expectations. Just viewing a child as moldable clay hardens the shell of his ego, for children both consciously and unconsciously desire to live up to adult expectations. As long as teachers ignore a child's Divine, creative capacity, they ignore his own inner experience. When educators discern the awesome creative force within children, they will awaken the Spirit of each child, rather than attempt to break it.

We admit that there are, and historically have been, significant barriers to elevating consciousness in our culture. The pearl of higher consciousness is always gained at a great price, for it requires a shift in orientation from tribal, unconscious thought to individual conscious thought. It requires living in the present rather than being obsessed by past or future. Unless we forfeit our old identity based on a limited, communal ego reality, we cannot embrace an identity founded on our inner genius, inner self-determination, and the use of our full creative intelligence.

Factory-style education that arose to serve the Industrial Revolution in 19th century America led to alienation and confusion in twentieth century schooling. As we begin the 21st century, we witness a new emphasis on testing, testing, testing, based on the desire to punish schools and teachers who fail to meet the arbitrary standards set by states and the federal government, according to which certan facts must be learned by a particular grade. We ignore the real child within, determined to indoctrinate him according to our warped materialistic values. Because of our misguided education, as much as any other factor, we are on the brink of exterminating our species.

Our schools have become youth camps devoted to conformity, to corporate and materialistic values. Our schools, therefore, like our corporate structures, are focused only on the exterior world. They ignore life within, the sleeping creative Being with so much promise and so little recognition. The same may be said with most of American culture, which values, above all, material wealth and the power of money, and which measures the value of human life by the "bottom line."

The Kingdom of Heaven is within you ... Seek ye first the Kingdom of Heaven and all things will be added unto you.

~Holy Bible [18]

Ever since the fifth century, our orthodox religions have declared that reliance on personal, inner knowledge or revelation is heresy, despite the fact that their founders (Abraham, Jesus, and Mohammad) found wisdom within and recommended that others look inward to find reality and wisdom. The Jewish Essenes and the Christian Gnostics who found wisdom and knowledge in this way were declared anathema by their orthodox, prosperous counterparts. In recent times, the two most remarkable discoveries of religious archaeology affirmed the primacy of inner life – the Nag Hammadi library of Gnostic writing (1,153 pages), and the Dead Sea Scrolls of Qumram of the Essenes, in 1945 and 1947, respectively. Due to the wrangling of scholars, most of whom represented orthodox Christianity, the translations of the Gnostic text were delayed for over thirty years. (The small portion of the 1,153 pages purchased by the Jung Institute was translated and presented to Jung on his 80th birthday).

The fate of the Dead Sea Scrolls was even worse. They were put in the hands of Christian scholars, and divided among them for translation. Only the least-significant scrolls have been translated; a single individual, Joseph Milik, who has since left the priesthood, refused to translate the most sensitive ones.

The Age of Enlightenment, with its absolute faith in human reason, believed the discoveries of science would rid the world of all evil. After Locke declared that knowledge is not innate, but comes only from observation of the external world governed by reason, other great figures deferred to his authority. School was seen as the vehicle to alter human nature by the application of rational thought. The instruction of the mind became the center of education. Man identified fully with the "rational" ego. Later, we will examine the ego more closely and see that the ego is anything but rational.

As our earth is devastated by man's greed, as our minds are ruled by our pathetic egos, as our country terrorizes in the name of anti-terrorism, as international corporations monopolize power and determine the scope and nature of education, we must see that only the application of universal spiritual principles will save our dying world. It is not our tradition of "family values" that will save us from ourselves. As the "radical" Jesus taught, *"and every one that hath forsaken houses, or brethren, or sisters, or father, or mother, or wife or children, or lands, for my name's sake, shall receive an hundredfold, and shall inherit everlasting life"* [Matthew: 19-29]

Only if our unconscious tradition of violence towards mother earth, women and children, and the compulsive need to do harm to our personal enemies (in business and economics, as well as life in general) yields to a new understanding – which is also an very ancient understanding – is there hope for the survival of our society.

Since the price of inner freedom includes a break with the destructive, unconscious group mind of our tribe, it requires that we think and decide for ourselves and assume responsibility for our thoughts and feelings, as well as our actions. Our individualization, our Naked Education, necessitates a collision with deeply entrenched, Western materialism because it elevates the primacy and power of inner Being over laws governing the behavior of material objects.

Commitment to our inner Being conflicts with the adoration of materialist culture and its own full set of societal values: to accumulate for oneself at the expense of others, to ostentatiously flaunt the wealth of one's home, one's car, one's job, the yacht for entertainment, to trust one's investment portfolio for security, and to insinuate one's status by the restaurants one frequents, the vacation resorts one jets to, marks a person as a success in this society.

For materialists, education in a prestigious school is an obvious road to fortune, rather than a pathway to understanding and compassion, for they can conceive only according to their awareness of what is most desirable.

We must admit that the challenge of raising consciousness over several millennia has been accepted only by the relatively few, and ignored by the masses. Despite the fact that well-recognized, enlightened leaders have, by their life and their teaching, consistently indicated that being born into a higher conscious life is available to all, this main message has been ignored. Abraham, Buddha, Jesus, and Mohammed – all taught what they lived: if one turned to the inner light of Being and followed its wisdom, one would embrace a powerful inner authority connected with Life. One would possess inner riches: Peace, Love, and Compassion for all.

Each of these enlightened men followed the small, still voice within and taught others to do the same, to give primacy to inner authority, and trust in inner direction.

Although you may follow in my footstep you must remember this "If your eyes are watching where I stepped then you will only see my path, what glorious wonder you shall never see till you look up and find your own path.

~Rev. Joseph Running Wolf Sparti [19]

Do not seek to follow in the footsteps of the wise. Seek what they sought.

~Basho [20]

We know the result for the masses. Institutionalized religions commandeered the authority to create the rules for their members to live by, pretending to serve as intermediaries between man and God, shamelessly claiming to be God's spokesmen. As a result, the overwhelming majority of individual men and women rejected their own inner guides and deferred to those with outward religious power. Human consciousness, as a whole, stagnated. The collective ego continued to rule the world by force and intimidation.

We must also acknowledge that since the Industrial Revolution, children have been deliberately trapped in schools at the lowest levels of consciousness so that, as adults, they might be fully exploited. From the introduction of compulsory education in Prussia in the 19th century to the present day, youngsters have been systematically trained to forsake their inner Being, their inner knowing, and conform to cruel expectations. In this process they have, for the most part, given away the possibility of becoming full human Beings.

Those who have been dispossessed of their true identity, sacrificed to a compulsory educational system of an industrialized society become adults who see totally through the ego's eyes. They tend to be unimaginative and conservative; they fanatically resist change, they dwell in the past and so shun life in the present. They have multiple addictions, although they would claim otherwise. Since they have been taught to interpret everything literally, they cannot understand life experiences, myths, dreams, poetry, drama, dance, art, and so reject or ignore the reality of inner Truth, Beauty, Peace, and Joy. As a result, they specialize in cynicism, hopelessness, pessimism, and materialism, although they would probably call themselves "realists." They are impressed by fame, power to control others, luxury, possessions, and money. They often hate their work, but see it as a necessary means to status and a comfortable life.

Naked Education, however, awakens students to consciousness of the fullness of life within and without.

Unlike the development of the body and its major systems, which tends to conform to a main sequence of unfolding, the flowering of consciousness may follow a number of radically different pathways. Each major avenue supports an entirely different way of knowing, a different reality.

Carl Jung has classified human Beings into a limited number of categories. If teachers become cognizant of these different types, each with a distinctive way of perceiving and learning, they can teach individual children much more effectively. If teachers consciously recognize their differences, they can and thus speak directly to their inner nature.

Carl Jung's typology of human personality fully illuminates the range and limits of awareness. Jung's determination to differentiate the ways in which consciousness manifests in individuals led him to combine – in different proportions – what he saw as the crucial forces that acted on the formation of character: two basic "attitudes" and the four "functions."

> *What Jung accomplished in Psychological Types was of twofold importance: he identified and described a number of basic psychological processes and he showed how these processes merged in various combinations to determine an individual's character. He set out to transform a general psychology of universal laws and processes into an individual psychology that described the unique characteristics and behavior of a specific person. The result was, as Jung said, a very practical psychology.*
>
> ~Calvin Hall and Vernon Nordby, *A Primer of Jungian Psychology* [22]

The two attitudes, according to Jung, refer to an individual's primary orientation to the world, either to objective reality or subjective reality.

Objective reality, composed of the objects in a person's environment, as well as the customs and conventions of the institutions of the society to which he belongs. Attention (energy) is invested in thoughts, perceptions, and feelings about objects in the environment. The extrovert is so obsessed with interacting with people and things that he disregards signals from his inner Being.

> *It is a fact of experience that the basic psychological functions seldom or never all have the same strength or degree of development in the same individual. As a rule, one or the other function predominates, in both strength and development. When thinking holds prior place among the psychological functions, i.e., when the life of the individual is mainly governed by reflective thinking so that every important action proceeds, or is intended to proceed, from intellectually considered motives, we may fairly call this a thinking type. Such a type may be either introverted or extroverted. We will first discuss the extroverted thinking type.*

This type will, by definition, be a man whose constant endeavor – in so far, of course, as he is a pure type – is to make all his activities dependent on intellectual conclusions, which in the last resort are always oriented by objective data, whether these be external facts or generally accepted ideas. This type of man elevates objective reality, or an objectively oriented intellectual formula, into the ruling principle not only for himself but for his whole environment. By this formula good and evil are measured, and beauty and ugliness determined. Everything that agrees with this formula is right, everything that contradicts it is wrong, and anything that passes by it indifferently is merely incidental. Because this formula seems to embody the entire meaning of life, it is made into a universal law which must be put into effect everywhere all the time, both individually and collectively. Just as the extroverted thinking type subordinates himself to his formula, so, for their own good, everybody around him must obey it too, for whoever refuses to obey it is wrong; he is resisting universal law, and is therefore unreasonable, immoral, and without a conscience. His moral code forbids him to tolerate exceptions; his ideal must under all circumstance be realized, for in his eyes it is the purest conceivable formulation of objective reality, and therefore, must also be a universally valid truth, quite indispensable for the salvation of mankind. This is not from any great love for his neighbor, but from the higher standpoint of justice and truth. Anything in his own nature that appears to invalidate this formula is a mere imperfection, an accidental failure, something to be eliminated on the next occasion, or, in the event of further failure, clearly pathological. If tolerance for the sick, the suffering, or the abnormal should chance to be an ingredient of the formula, special provisions will be made for humane societies, hospitals, prisons, missions, etc., or at least extensive plans will be drawn up.

But the more rigid the formula, the more he develops into a martinet, a quibbler, and a prig, who would like to force himself and others into one mould. Here we have the two extremes between which the majority of these type move.

The fact that an intellectual formula never has been and never will be devised which could embrace and express the manifold possibilities of life must lead to the inhibition or exclusion of other activities and ways of living that are just as important. In the first place, all those activities that are dependent on feeling will become repressed in such a type – for instance, aesthetic activities, taste, artistic sense, cultivation of friends, etc. Irrational phenomena such as religious experiences, passions, and such like are often repressed to the point of complete unconsciousness. Doubtless there are exceptional people who are able to sacrifice their entire life to a particular formula, but for most of us such exclusiveness is impossible in the long run. Sooner or later, depending on outer circumstances or inner disposition, the potentialities repressed by the intellectual attitude will make themselves indirectly felt by disturbing the conscious conduct of life. When the disturbance reaches a definite pitch, we speak of neurosis. In most cases it does not go so far, because the individual instinctively allows himself extenuating modifications of his formula in a suitably rationalistic guise, thus creating a safety value.

~Carl Jung, *Psychological Types, P.346-348* [23]

Subjective reality of psychic events is invisible to an observer and private in nature. Energy is channeled into subjective psychic complexes and processes, and importance given to symbolic forms of expression. Exploration of the inner world, which may be assumed to be as vast and varied as the external universe, takes precedence. To others, an introvert often appears to be aloof, anti-social, and shy owing to his preoccupation with internal interests and his indifference to objective reality.

Objective and subjective attitudes may alternate, on specific occasions, but they do not mix. Consciousness takes only one form at a time. One tends, however, to have a definite preference of perspective throughout a lifetime. Therefore, one may be defined, for practical purposes, as either an extrovert or introvert.

According to Jung's principle of psychic compensation, the conscious extrovert is unconsciously and introvert – for example, in dream life or when taken over by uncharacteristic behavior. In a similar way, a conscious introvert will unconsciously express his repressed extroversion.

Interwoven with the two attitudes of extroversion and introversion are what Jung called the four functions, the four ways of relating to our reality. Jung paired the functions of thinking and feeling and also the functions he also paired of sensation and intuition. In each individual, one of these four avenues of relating to our world will dominate his attention. That is, he will specialize in one main way of apprehending his reality; he will predictably contact one main function – thinking or feeling or sensation or intuition – for gaining information about his world.

If our consciousness follows a thinking track, our attention is given to ideas, and rarely given to our feelings. If feeling predominates, our least-developed function is thinking. On the other hand, if our preferred means of gaining information is through our five body senses, we are primarily tuned into sensations, and have an undeveloped intuition. If our intuition is our primary function, we tend to be oblivious to information from our senses, but hypersensitive to intuitive messages.

A thinker will predictably avoid feelings. A master of feelings avoids logical thinking. An intuitive is relatively oblivious to his body senses. And a sensation type has very little intuitive ability. One's favorite form of gaining information about the world automatically decides one's most neglected function.

And so, as our attention is directed to one preferred function, its pair automatically creates a blind spot in its opposite function. That leaves two other functions, which Jung called secondary or tertiary to the main functions, to serve us when the primary function temporarily fails to dominate.

The combination of two attitudes and the four main functions creates eight main personality types. Add the particular secondary and tertiary functions and the variable strengths of each function, and the possible combinations are legion. But a look at the eight main types is itself illuminating, and provides a sense of the human variety in the most basic orientation to life. It also lets us appreciate that an individual's consciousness is directed in only one of eight main possible ways, so that there are eight main forms of human consciousness on earth given to eight different ways of focusing on reality, or eight sides of the same reality. Like the story of eight men each in contact with a different part of the proverbial elephant, each having his own interpretation of the reality of the beast, unable to resolve their differences, we, today, struggle to understand each other's perspective, each other's truth, because each of us naturally prefers to be a specialist in one type of information.

Yet today we demand strict standardization in the education of our children, to the detriment of the majority. The psychological type most in tune with our system of schooling is the extroverted, thinking type. We will explore that type, and then summarize the seven remaining types. Remember, each of these brief portraits represents the more obvious cases in which the attitude is well developed while the opposite function is especially undeveloped or absent.

Although Carl Jung wrote much about the universal, common elements of people, he saw, as well, the key elements that differentiate us and strongly color our personality. Jung's presentation of personality topology illuminated and clarified our essential differences. His model of personality types has been changed and popularized today in the Briggs-Myers personality types. In the process, Jung's insights into the differentiation of conscious and unconscious forces on personality have been sacrificed, as have the dynamics between the principal function and the auxiliary functions. In my view, it is most helpful for educational purposes to follow Jung's personality types.

Jung points out that the ideal, in terms of human consciousness, would be for each person to have attitudes of extroversion and introversion in equal strength, and to equally balance the four functions of thinking, feeling, sensation, and intuition. To have direct access to both inner and outer worlds and to the wealth of information from the realms of thinking, feeling, sensation and intuition would, in a totally integrated individual, produce a kind of superman or superwoman with remarkable, godlike powers. Such a person would be in tune with what the ordinary person would consider impossible. For most of us, our limited orientation places our ego more in the dark that in the light, seeing but a small part of the larger picture.

I have added a few observations of my own to Jung's descriptions of the eight types.

A. Extroverted Thinking Type

[Attention is primarily given to Thinking about objective reality]

This type may, in its idealized form, be represented by the scientist who seeks an understanding of external Nature and her laws, and applies a theoretical structure with which to organize his findings. It is a Charles Darwin-like figure, an extroverted thinker with feelings somewhat repressed, appearing impersonal, even aloof and arrogant. In most people, however, extroverted thinking lacks the clarity of a mature scientist; most might be described as banal and redundant. This imitative thinker, however, still supports, at all costs, the independence of the external universe, and tends to lose consciousness of his inner emotions because of his extraordinary focus on external objects. An individual whose emotions are fully unconscious will show definite negative signs: he may appear to be tyrannical, superstitious, insensitive, bigoted, and sterile in thought; as the opposite of the true scientist, he may take on the characteristics of the mad scientist.

This type is fit by nature to become the ideal student in an educational system modeled entirely on a preference for extroverted thinking and objective reality. Such a system requires all of its students to memorize a set curriculum that stresses scientific information, facts, and definitions that represent only one aspect of reality. When schools indoctrinate all students into the absolute truth of science, they are not educating, but brainwashing. Education, in our view, should broaden rather then narrow our perspective, balance our extravagances, widen our vision, and call forth additional inner resources.

Jung's description of the extroverted thinker given above is, at the same time, an accurate description of the mainstream school in America, not by coincidence.

Jung's scientific thinker, like our highly prejudiced school systems, insists on a single view of reality. The young scientific thinker represents a single portrait of the ideal student as the successful academic. In our school systems, the reality and value of other personality types is either ignored or patronized by allowing limited non-academic courses that tend to be regarded as of lesser value than their more prestigious, academic counterparts.

B. Extroverted Feeling Type

[Attention is given primarily to Feelings about objects, people, and cultural values]

Most often female, these individuals are guided by their feelings. For these people, feelings are under conscious control and are personal in nature. They harmonize with objective situations and societal values. A woman's choice for a mate to love tends to be reasonable, suitable, and respectable; yet, remarkably, her love appears genuine. She only permits herself to think what is in accord with her feelings. Everything that falls under the spell of traditional values is cherished; she totally dismisses all else. She considers that something is "good" or "beautiful" not because she has that subjective impression of it (she does not!), but because it seems appropriate to value it and treat it so. This type obeys fashion, flocks to church, to the theater, to concerts, merely because such actions follow generally well-regarded standards of behavior. It is the nature of extroverted feeling individuals to actively support beliefs about what is considered socially acceptable. These people infuse harmony into social life.

From the outside, her thinking may appear whimsical, infantile, negative, or contradictory, because with this type thinking always accommodates itself to the current feeling. But if her feelings become exaggerated or extreme and control her absolutely, she acts cold, fickle, or hysterical. Then her gushing talk and extravagant displays of emotion ring hollow. Although she tends to become attached to people, her allegiance can immediately be overturned if her feelings change; her love can rapidly turn to hate.

C. Extroverted, Sensation Type

[Attention is given primarily to the Sensations of objects, people, and cultural values]

Commonly men, these people love to accumulate facts about the external environment. They are realistic, factual, and practical, and not particularly concerned with the meaning of events. Any thought or feeling reduces to objective causes. One's life, therefore, revolves around an accumulation of things and experiences. Usually jolly, their aim is refined enjoyment and good company; their morality provides for that. The feeling life may be very shallow. They are attracted to experiences of danger and pleasure.

These people live for the sensations provided by life experiences (except for subjective sensations, which are repressed.) They have a strong sensuous tie to concrete objects that intensely excite their senses. Although they are often seen as very rational because their focus is completely on objects of the "real" world, they pay little attention to reason or logic. But they are masters at differentiating sensations, and so appreciate aesthetic purity, fine food and drink, fine clothes, and fine cars. Often jovial, with no desire to dominate others, they are suspicious of the subjective world and its "dark" thoughts, feelings, and intuitions.

But when sensations overwhelm all other functions, this type turns negative and becomes bound to objects, and compulsive about pleasure seeking. They become jealous and develop phobias. They make absurd assumptions, develop a punctilious morality, or turn to hair-splitting pedantry or dreary moralizing. Then they can be mean as well. Then they display multiple addictions and compulsions.

D. Extroverted, Intuitive Type

[Attention is given primarily to Intuitions about current or new possibilities in the external world]

Commonly women, these people are often unstable and capricious. Unable to maintain interest in anything for long, they follow their intuition wherever it leads. Novelty is their oyster. Although they enter new relationships with eagerness, they often seem irresponsible as friends. Flitting from hobby to hobby, or job to job, they are quickly bored and will, without a thought, abandon what only yesterday enchanted them.

The intuitive has a nose for new possibilities; stability and ordinariness suffocate her. Whatever offers current, unlimited promise is quickly seized upon, but soon becomes a prison or a poison. Neither thinking nor feeling have any force with her. Judgment is thrown to the winds. Loyalty to the compulsion of the new vision causes everything else to vanish. A master at exploiting every social situation, of making crucial connections with prospective movers and shakers, such types are especially fit for economic and social projects. She can inspire enthusiasm and courage in others and can successfully jump-start a new venture.

E. Introverted. Thinking Type

[Attention is given primarily to Thinking about the inner world of ideas, symbols, and images]

Represented by the philosopher or existential psychologist, the introverted thinker is on a quest to get to the bottom of his own nature. In extreme cases, this may drive him to become schizophrenic. Like his extroverted thinking counterpart, who also fears emotions, he may appear distant and unemotional, one who does not value people. This type needs extended periods to escape from the crowd, to be alone to recharge his energy.

He follows his own thinking, even when his ideas are ridiculed by others. As a result, he is able to find practical or theoretical solutions to a wide range of problems. He can be very independent and often refuses outside help. Apt to appear stubborn, arrogant, and thoughtless, he can seem unapproachable or hostile. If feeling is totally suppressed, he will become unstable and reckless.

F. Introverted Feeling Type

[Attention is given primarily to Feelings about one's inner life]

These are more often women who keep their feelings well hidden from others. Therefore, others experience them as remote, as loners. They are hard to read because they tend to be taciturn, unapproachable, mysterious. Although they often seem sad or depressed, they nevertheless possess an inner equanimity, a serenity, and self-sufficiency like the introverted thinking type. They have the power to comfort themselves. They use their feelings as a rudder to guide their path in life, irrespective of the actions or rationalizations of others, and, in that way, follow their own star. They rarely open up because they fear that if they do so, they will dissipate their power. Occasionally, they erupt with emotional intensity and shock their family or friends, who were unaware that anything was disturbing them. They can be charismatic in a quiet manner.

G. Introverted Sensation Type

[Attention is given primarily to Sensations arising in the inner world]

The allurements of the world cannot compete with the intense inner sensations of this type. Straightforward verbal communication is often awkward and frustrating; artistic expression is easier, although the art produced is not usually regarded as compelling by others. This type appears self possessed, sometimes even passive and rigid, unable to fully engage life. Because he is cut off from the objective world as well as from subjective intuition, he often appears to be at odds with himself and others, and has a difficult time fitting in socially. This causes extreme isolation from others, which oppresses him. He may bore others because of his paucity of thought and his lack of emotional clarity.

H. Introverted, Intuitive Type

[Attention is given primarily to one's unique Intuitive insights]

The true artist represents this type, as well as visionaries and eccentrics. Appearing as an enigma to others, he himself feels misunderstood and unappreciated. Ignoring conventions and external reality, he has difficulty communicating with others. Isolated in his incomprehensible world of primordial images, he often lacks the discipline to track and interpret the images and archetypes of his unconscious. Like the introverted sensation type, he may have no close friends, yet his intuition to follow his own drummer often works for him.

Although many children's personalities are blends of the 16 types derived by Jung (as he acknowledged), in my experience, others conformed closely to the pure types, and so had more than theoretical value for us.

At The Well, personality types served as tools to help us recognize the different realities in which our students lived, and suggested untold ways to support them in their efforts.

In a society whose values celebrate the open recognition of external reality and the clear distrust and denial of the subjective world, whose institutions, political leaders, and celebrities are strongly extroverted, introverts often find it difficult to be validated by others. Yet all children (and adults) crave attention from others. In a large school setting, where the competition for attention from students and teachers is fierce, where the curriculum dotes on the outer world as its darling, the more aggressive extroverts dominate the school scene.

The fact that traditional school systems in the West is geared to only one of the eight types should give us pause to reconsider if one standardized system is a sane, rational approach. While one-eighth of the students find the curriculum extremely palatable and have many of their basic preferences met, the others often become second-class citizens, without support for their form of conscious awareness, and without the tools to compete in such a system. While the large schools claim to be economically efficient, it is difficult, from the point of view of personal development, to imagine a more inefficient and destructive approach to teaching and learning.

In our observation, school is a breeze for extroverted thinkers, and accords with their natural strengths. Tests are easy for them. Memorizing facts is relatively easy – they hardly need to study. Even those who pay little attention in class score very high on standardized, multiple-choice tests.

But extroverted thinkers are not in need of more and more thinking, of text books crammed with tens of thousands of pages of facts, formulae, and information concerning English, American history, earth science, astronomy, biology, chemistry, botany, physics, pre-algebra, algebra, geometry, and calculus, and thousands of definitions to be ingested with little or no creative thought involved.

Even thinkers do not benefit by constant thinking. As Jung observed, for consciousness to develop in each personality, the dominant function needs to be balanced by the development of other functions. In his lectures to teachers, he was especially concerned that care be taken that the extroverted thinker be protected from excessive thinking by developing his feeling function to counterbalance a tendency to compulsive thought. One who cannot stop thinking is cut off from true creative thought which requires, as well as the thinking component, the ability to enter into silence and experience the present moment. Inspiration requires contact with inner being.

For the majority of youngsters who are not thinking types, intellectual learning, unrelated to the life force within, unrelated to crucial inner needs, simply rejects Spirit as it undermines the sacredness of life. For the majority, intellectual learning serves only to harden the shell of the ego. Too much intellectual stimulation separates the student from connection with his own Being, so that he becomes incapable of knowing directly. His knowing becomes brittle, lifeless, abstract and dry.

With the timeless dimension comes a different kind of knowing, one that does not "kill" the Spirit that lives within every creature and every thing. A knowing that does not destroy the sacredness of the mystery of life but contains a deep love and reverence for all that is. A knowing of which the mind knows nothing.

The mind cannot know the tree. It can only know facts or information about the tree. My mind cannot know you, only labels, judgments, facts, and opinions about you. Being alone knows directly.

There is a place for mind and mind knowledge. It is in the practical realm of day-to-day living. However, when it takes over all aspects of your life, including your relationships with other human beings and with nature, it becomes a monstrous parasite that, unchecked, may well end up killing all life on the planet and finally itself by killing its host.

~Eckhart Tolle, *The Power of Now* [17]

Direct knowing is a product of one's inner nature. Children are naturally connected to their inner Being, but in the course of being conditioned at home or in school, gradually relinquish their ability to live in the present moment. Instead, they learn to be controlled by guilt from the past and anticipation of future events or possessions.

Only the ability to live in the now allows the life force to flow unimpeded. This flow naturally creates direct knowledge, which tends to be simple and unerring. The animating presence of life within is clearly felt as arising within the inner body – not in the various organs in a literal sense – but in the space within the body filled with a consciousness of "I Am."

At a young age, a child calls himself by his name, rather than the "I" or "me" familiar to the adult, signifying that he has not yet identified with the ego. Young children experience having the center of their Being inside their entire body, as may any adult who takes care to live in present time.

But when ego is strengthened in the early years, a child learns to avoid life in the now because, more than anything else, ego desires separation and an independent existence. That is accomplished only by creating a distance, a disassociation from all other beings. Ego quickly becomes a master of living in the past and anticipating the future, escaping the present moment. Ego escapes present reality and compulsively uses it only as a means to obtain desirable ego ends. The present becomes subservient to an illusory future; ego never bathes in the perfection of the present.

With constant encouragement from parents and teachers to be guilty for past mistakes and to anticipate future goals, children's experiences of living in the present often fade into the background of memory as they age.

Some children, we have noticed, retain an ability to enter the present at will, or to live almost entirely in the present. They often have well-developed egos but preserve their ability to be fully present, connected to truth in the now. Their ability to frequently reside in the present and occasionally visit past or future is analogous to a bi-lingual child switching back and forth between languages; she automatically responds fully to a new frame of reference.

Of course, adults also vary in their ability to be present, but it is a rare adult who can turn off his mind and surrender to silence. For the most part, adults have lost touch with the inner life of their Beings; they no longer receive messages from their higher Self, and no longer remember when they did. Those who have submerged their consciousness in the ego world have forfeited their inner sight.

Whenever the mind stops, inner awareness explodes into life. An artist lost in the object she is painting follows line and apprehends color without thought of whether she is succeeding or not. By developing intense present focus, she avoids being under the control of ego; ego consciousness destroys creativity by labeling, by criticizing, by judging, by inhibiting. The successful artist simply enjoys the experience of creating in the moment.

In our experience at The Well School, most children who draw – not to impress, but to express – are able to concentrate for long stretches of time even though their Being is unaware of time passing, for the experience of the Now is out of time. Similarly those who become self-absorbed in music, drama, dance, pottery, ceramics, batik, weaving, are able to experience, for significant portions of their life, working directly from their inner Being. They can reject the clock because they have surrendered to the activity; they can overcome self-criticism because they have surrendered to their joy.

At The Well, we built upon activities that children naturally loved, often working together as an extended family on many projects. In this milieu, we took advantage of the perspectives of a variety of personality types represented in most groupings of children.

We sought, whenever possible, to have all of our students participate in all the activities and studies, for we saw that every child needed to develop all sides of his nature (all his functions, in Jungian terms). So all students sang together, danced together. We involved all in theater, meditation, yoga, aerobics, martial arts, daily jobs, foreign languages, soccer, hockey, and basketball. Our slogan, "Everybody does everything," meant that it was a school expectation for students to fully participate in activities whether they loved them or not, whether they were good at them or not. And we asked them to do it with gusto.

The Plains Indians of the American West recognized a crucial truth: the highest achievement in life is to become a true human Being, in touch with one's inner Being and attuned to the natural world. We are each born with that potential, but we need, before it can be individually fulfilled, to drop our resistance to life and cooperate with natural life forces. Only then are we free to discover and uncover our inner Being. These Native Americans knew the path to humanness required a process that involved creating a new identity separate from the one given by one's family at birth, an identity based on a clear recognition of the primacy of one's inner resources.

In Native American plains society, adolescents were expected to experience a re-birth during their vision quest. And they did so or became recognized as deficient human Beings. The single requirement for claiming to be a human being was a consciousness of a new, individual Self. One was expected, thereafter, to follow and express one's own, individual identity. One was expected to focus on private, inner communication as well as to cooperate with spiritual entities. This consciousness was marked by its distinguishing features:

★ Contact with the visible and invisible world Spirit

★ Compassion for the Spirit of all living things

★ Responsibility to protect the exquisite, living environment

In subscribing to the crucial role of consciousness in the evolution of mankind, we subscribe, as well, to this Native American teaching about the nature of human Beings. Consciousness, in our view, determines our poverty or our riches, our negative effects on others or our ability to transmit love, peace, and wisdom.

Heightened awareness has little standing in present Western society, that same society that, as a whole, attempted or fully succeeded in committing genocide against Native Americans. For Toni and me, becoming full human Beings has been our constant aspiration. In our own heart, it represents an ideal we strive for every day.

Our own heart always exceeds us.

~Rainer Maria Rilke [24]

The Native American expectation of being *reborn* is, in many ways, similar to what Carl Jung called *individuation*, the giving up of the old, collective identity based on irrational fears of the ego concerning vulnerability and death, in favor of the gradual adoption of a new identity based on the discovery of inner life resources. This process helps confront and integrate the unconscious forces which move us.

If our world is to survive and continue to provide a home for mankind, we must stop training children to become cogs in the insane corporate machinery that is systematically destroying the precious environment and the beautiful natural world as a whole.

We believe it is crucial for educators of the young to see the creative genius in every child, to implicitly know that behind the ego identity of every youngster, which reveals selfish pre-occupations and a will to power over others, lies a divine Being. In our view, it is the sacred duty of the authentic teacher to create, out of his own Being, a relationship with both the inner Self and outer ego identity of each child, so as not to unconsciously react to any selfish habits he may have.

Unless the teacher defines her relationship with each child as a sacred interchange, she will, by default, enter relationships based on intellectual and emotional reactions – ego prejudice. It is all too human to fruitlessly respond to ego demands of another and ignore the living, Divine aspects, and in so doing, dramatically obfuscate life within.

It is vital to remember that even the child who has already separated himself and prematurely appears as a fearful, isolated self, has a fuller, deeper sacred Being tucked away. Naked Education may reacquaint him with his larger Self, widen his consciousness, and connect him with his creativity, vulnerability, and compassion. It may awaken him to his essence that he had forgotten. He may reflect in the lost facets of his gemlike Self, the light from within.

The exclusive aspect of personality, the part that wants to be superior to others and dominate them, that part that separates from life and identifies with materiality and death, the part that needs to win, needs to be right, needs to judge, needs to undermine, needs to control his environment and limit the personality, is known universally as the "ego."

Freud dubbed it ego and thus, intentionally or not, identified it with the self. According to this revered man, however, who brilliantly and in detail described the ego's arsenal of weapons which he called "defenses," the ego cannot stand the truth about itself. It compulsively employs its unconscious defenses to deflect and deny its negative qualities. Ego to its core is a liar and a cheat, a deceiver, a chauvinist, one who endlessly places responsibility for its decisions and actions on people and circumstances in the past and present, one who avoids experience by becoming rigid.

Ego's favorite methods for avoiding simple truth and experience, reveal its unconscious cleverness, deception, falsehood, and inauthenticity. The ego defenses according to Freud are:

✖ **Denial**. Refusing to admit that something unpleasant or taboo is happening. When feelings cause anxiety or guilty, they are denied and stored in the unconscious mind.

✖ **Repression.** Blocking a threatening idea, memory, or emotion from consciousness. Whatever truth makes it uncomfortable, it defiantly forgets and denies.

✖ **Projection.** Ego projects onto others (as a camera projects the image of a frame of film upon a screen) what it hates in itself.

✖ **Reaction Formation** Ego often claims the exact opposite of its true feelings.

✖ **Fixation** When ego experiences frustration, it refuses to participate in exploration. It simply digs in its heels and gets angry and ugly.

✖ **Regression**. If ego does not get its way, it reverts to immaturity.

Ego seeks to single-handedly commandeer and control the ship of personality, for ego is blind to the importance and usefulness of all other aspects of the greater Self. The ego is a loner who determines the destination, sets the course, and ignores any intelligence or direction from outside its limited view. Ego denies and excludes the largest part of the personality, the unconscious, as well as its shadow self, its anima or animus, and its wealth of archetypes: symbolic images representing universal experience. In a consistent attempt to deny and project what it fears and condemns in itself, ego's chief concern is to appear, to itself and others, as innocent and good. Its head in the sand approach rebuffs consciousness.

The single, most influential factor in determining the degree of consciousness in an individual is whether or not the person has totally identified with a false ego self that diminishes the personality as a whole while denying its living Divine aspects.

In Book 5 of our series on *Naked Education: The Self as the Center of Education*, we will explore, in detail, the strategies ego uses to bolster itself in the face of competition with others – to the detriment of the personality as a whole. We will also examine how the full personality can flourish under the great intelligence and influence of the inner Self. If man is to survive his compulsive overindulgence in thinking and destroying whatever he hates, the next step in evolution requires dis-identifying with the ego and identifying with the true Self. Only in this way will education serve an authentic mission: to work with each child to raise consciousness, to reconcile the warring forces within him, and to provide legitimate avenues to integrate and express creative forces.

How does consciousness usually develop? How does a larger identity emerge? By centering one's identity in the heart rather than in the mind. By accepting what the heart reveals whether it is positive or negative.

Significant individual growth in consciousness begins when we face, rather than deny, what C. G. Jung called our "shadow," the hidden, politically incorrect part of our nature that we fear to reveal or acknowledge, thinking that in doing so will cause rejection by self, by family, by friends, and by our society at large. Jung saw that when we incorporate, rather than reject, our "negative" qualities, a wondrous transformation occurs. Our acceptance releases tremendous positive energy for our personality to utilize. We all know this truth from the symbolic story of "Beauty and the Beast;" when Beauty gives her heart to the Beast and embraces and accepts its ugliness, he is transformed from a monster into a prince.

The next step in transformation often comes from dealing with conscious and unconscious wisdom through the medium of myth, sacred texts from around the world, literature, art, poetry, and dreams. As a class, we at The Well recognize – make conscious through discussion – in detail the literal story line, and then the underlying theme or motif, and the spiritual principles at work in these mediums. In mythology, we find everywhere symbolic truth about human nature in general. In sacred texts, in great literature and art, we find inspired messages. In dreams, we discover messages of our own unconscious wisdom and notice they are at odds with the distorted reality of our ego. When the insight of the unconscious is brought to light and used to counterbalance and correct the waking conclusions that ego has formed, we open to a wider perspective, and see new solutions.

A major leap in consciousness comes when we identify with the Self, our true Being, the spark of the omnipotent and omniscient Divine within us. At first we work blindly, even unconsciously, focusing our attention on Self as we become more and more conscious of its existence. When Self is recognized as the central, organizing principle, the hub of the personality, it is able to effect great changes. Self, as Jung noted, has the power to reconcile warring forces within the personality, and create from the integration of the opposites, new positive powers. Furthermore, Self can harmonize and integrate all the aspects of the personality, and bring peace to a beleaguered Soul. Self can serve as an organizing and harmonizing central sun to the planets (aspects) of our solar system (personality).

The recognition of the shadow, the use of stories, poems, art, and dreams to explore the powers of the unconscious, and the recognition of the Self were not abstractions to Toni and me, for we had worked, throughout the years, with all of these. Our challenge at The Well was to make these techniques for personal growth available, at appropriate moments, to our students.

Jung considered the "individuation" of the personality the chief purpose of each individual life. Individuation was a lifetime process of awakening to the subtle forces of our Self and of the universe, and learning to work with them to transform and understand one's life. Such a journey means constantly enlarging one's perspective in order to transcend personal fears and then to serve, in love, for the good of all mankind and for the planet as a living whole.

Individuation does not lead to men becoming robots, doing and thinking according to a set pattern, but demands, instead, that each person find his individual way of working with psychic powers, his unique way of expressing his ever-expanding consciousness. It is an unfoldment, under the control of no man, no government, no religious or educational institution, one which relies on the development of individual understanding, individual forgiveness of the past, and a heightened individual vision. In other words, the process of individuation gives power, accountability, and responsibility to the individual, who, under the guidance of the inner Self and in conscious communication with his own Being, becomes the custodian of awareness for the entire personality.

In the process the Self is consciously empowered as it withdraws dependence on outer authority: institutions, corporations, and collective values. Although it seems to be Nature's plan for human Beings to acquire great awareness through learning how to communicate with Self and inner Being, the institutions of our civilization, including our educational institutions, oppose the development of individual choice and responsibility by assuming control and authority over young people, and imposing restrictive regulations in order to control their thinking and behavior and restrict their development.

The most efficient, most effective education in this country occurred in the 17th and early 18th century, when schooling was arranged by individuals (mostly home schooling and tutoring), and when formal schooling was spontaneously limited to one or two years of formal study. The population's literacy rate approached 100 percent before compulsory education was initiated state by state during the second half of the 18th century and the first half of the 19th century. The longer compulsory education has been in effect, the worse the educational consequences for students, yet the myth persists that forced education is a great benefit to society. Governing institutions that increase their own power by co-opting the sacred power of individuals will not cede their power willingly.

Before compulsory education dominated our country, for roughly 200 years, the majority of colonists and early Americans read books that many college graduates cannot comprehend today. Yet, the general perception today, fostered by our institutions, is that 12 years of a compulsory education, although hostile to the development of consciousness, should stand as the mandatory school experience for most children.

At The Well School, our commitment to conscious education has only grown stronger. The creativity and enthusiasm of our students, as well as their willingness to take on extensive responsibility, spoke to us of its success. Teachers (without teaching certificates) and students dedicated to self-knowledge demonstrated remarkable wisdom, as well as academic proficiency and depth. Familiarity with simple techniques of focus and attention did not limit academic attainment, but spurred and enhanced it.

While far-ranging experience made it possible:

> *I stepped from plank to plank*
> *So slow and cautiously*
> *The stars about my head I felt,*
> *About my feet the sea.*
>
> *I knew not but the next*
> *Would be my final inch, –*
> *This gave me that precarious gain*
> *Some call experience.*

~Emily Dickinson [25]

Students who were in touch with their inner resources had a greater curiosity about and a better grasp of objective reality; they also experienced how the inner and outer worlds were interrelated.

> *I had six honest serving men – they taught me all I know: There names were*
> *Where and What and When and Why and How and Who.*

> ~Rudyard Kipling [26]

As educators, we hold, therefore, that it is our duty to lift our own consciousness, to face and admit our own darkness, that we might be enlivened and enlightened. It is our task to help each student to confront his shadow in order that he become more realistic (less inflated), more powerful (less intimidated), and more forgiving (less judgmental of self and others). Another way to say this is that the personality must be enlarged to accept its so-called "bad" characteristics, so that it will become, as a result, more positive and energized, more in tune with its inner Being. Repression and intimidation are never answers. Integration into a larger whole is.

It is also essential for each student to become aware of her unconscious nature and her sacred inner Being. It is through this expansion of consciousness that the primacy of the ego fades as the inner Self gains ascendancy.

The ego's understanding is limited; its intelligence can be best used for gaining information, for organizing, and for discharging practical matters. As a servant to the greater personality it has a crucial role in the health of the whole individual, attending to a multitude of practical matters. For full functioning of the personality ego must complement the inner Self:

> *Things unseen have a light of their own.*

> ~Raoul Plus, *Living with God* [27]

A far greater intelligence resides in the inner Self, for it has access to universal knowledge. It is capable of discerning the invisible as well as the visible, of knowing intuitively its full potential, of revealing the Divine qualities which lie at the core of its Being: Unconditional Love, Peace, Wisdom, Trust in the universe, and Compassion for all.

The real test of a man is not what he knows, but what he is in himself and his relations to others.

~Alfred Lord Tennyson [28]

The foundation of Naked Education does not rest on the conventional wisdom of the past. It does not subscribe to the false securities of the ego: to unquestioned dogma; to absolute authority; to worldly, Machiavellian principles calculated to advance ego aggrandizement; or to religious rules designed to maintain the innocence of youth through unthinking obedience to the church. All these avenues do not lead to wisdom because they ignore the central struggle of life: to raise consciousness and find within one's Self the source of Truth, of Light, of Love.

The goal of Naked Education is individual birth into a greater reality. Every student is called on to transform his ego-based reality by learning to intimately know his lower nature, to recognize his greater Self within, and to seek direction from an individualized Self in tune with the universe.

How can this happen for young children?

Through a community that awakens consciousness by regularly discussing the nitty gritty of everyday life as well as the potential of each individual to shine, transformations occur. To become aware of the tension (disparity) between our actual behavior and our inherent possibilities, to hold that disparity clearly in consciousness, itself generates a natural tension, which automatically shrinks the distance between the actual and the potential, bringing us closer to our genius.

Naked Education is not for the weak-hearted, for it is, by design, replete with challenges, as we shall see in later chapters, and dependent both on a student's willingness to transcend himself or herself, and a teacher's willingness to do the same.

If the doors of perception were cleansed everything would appear to man as it is: infinite. For man has closed himself up, till he sees all things thro' narrow chinks of his cavern.

~William Blake, *The Marriage of Heaven and Hell* [29]

Consciousness does not expand of itself; it does not grow, as the body of a child might, just because time passes. It requires a shift of perception to graduate from the smaller idea of what one can comfortably do, to an expanded view that allows students to dare to prove their ability to do what they once considered impossible. Rarely do students fail in this process, unless their parents continually call into question the challenges set before them. Sometimes, without parental support, students still succeed beyond their parents' expectations. And sometimes they believe, with their parents, that they are personally limited and cannot accomplish the "inconceivable."

Because Toni and I believed it was our essential task in life to outgrow our limitations and raise our consciousness, we did not balk at asking the same of our students. We knew from our experience that the growth process requires respect and patience, that it often cannot be forced. We recognized that we could not compel a student to develop consciousness; nor was there any way to accomplish it for them. But, we believed every individual had a powerful, inner need to realize his potential, and out of that need, came the will to do it.

Schools and teachers can effectively indoctrinate students, but neither schools nor teachers can, of themselves, create awareness in their students, because consciousness requires full inner, individual assent.

What our school did to prepare students to dare to take risks was to ask them to take full responsibility for their life situation. We wove a school environment from the nine strands of our deepest commitments.

Governing the Life of our School were these 9 principles:

1. Present, on a regular basis, symbolic literature that resonates with universal truths, and which portrays, for those with insight, the conflicts between lower and higher levels of consciousness.

Experience is a jewel, and it need be so, for it is often purchased at an infinite rate.

~William Shakespeare [30]

2. Provide a forum to regularly and openly discuss what is usually forbidden in schools: all aspects of our experiences as individuals on earth, including our thoughts, our emotions, our sensations, and our intuitions. We encouraged students, within a framework of respect and decency, to express honest, straightforward discord or love for one another; to attempt to understand each other; to request changes of behavior from each other in order to seek resolution. Toni and I felt that Life brought particular people (students, teachers, parents, and friends) together to learn from each other, and we used our school as a vehicle to pursue the greatest possible learning for the greatest number of

people. Much significant learning, in this respect, occurred at Class Meeting. (A full description of our Class Meetings appears in Book One of this series.)

3. Discuss a variety of paradigms for personal growth to make students aware of the possibilities of people to change and grow. In that context, we also discussed the significant levels of pain in individual lives, and the importance of recognizing and confronting painful life experiences in order to grow in consciousness and deal with the real world. We encouraged students and teachers in our school community to be able to voice their experiences of inner conflict, fear, and pain, or their experiences of transcendence that lifted them to a new consciousness. Our dialogue often incorporated descriptions of ego reality and ego behavior, and the possibilities of focusing on a different center in oneself. Through our interactions, our intent was to show respect for all.

Our thirty-four years of teaching at The Well demonstrated to us that Naked Education is not an ivory tower that excludes the unpleasant but real challenges of life, but a fiery cauldron that demands new decisions which may radically alter one's life and one's outlook. As a school, we dealt every day with both individual and collective pain by acknowledging its existence and addressing it.

Life for a student in any school, including our own, is never one smooth ride. Although the issues we confronted might seem unimportant by adult standards, each angry ego, as is always the case, inflicted significant pain, whether students hid the ache or consciously dealt with it. Jealousies, one-upmanship contests, passive or active resistance to the wishes of others, confrontations and barbs, competition over friends – each upsetting interchange released poison into the environment and undermined confidence. Yet, by addressing the pain, we learned together to deal with what had been created in our environment, and accepted responsibility for our individual and collective words and acts. Ignoring pain (the usual response of an educational system) only gives it deadly, unconscious power. Dealing with it not only necessitates facing and overcoming the terror in our lives, but also the process of bringing light into the darkness. That is how a family or a community can heal its individual and collective pain.

Open experience of emotional pain presented a great opportunity as well. It often served as a choice point for those who had a degree of awareness, a chance to observe and learn from one's pain rather than just react to it and set off another round of poisoning. When faced with the emotional pain caused by ego attachment, one can, at the same moment, deal directly with the accumulative body of pain from the past. Each time one experiences intense discomfort, or frustrating stagnation, a grand opportunity exists for growth, for by choosing to move beyond the ego orientation that caused the pain, we were able to explore higher perspectives.

When a school directly addresses the pain that lives in its students, teachers, and parents on a regular basis, the opportunities for a transformation of bitter relationships and petty jealousies are legion. But when a school ignores the presence of deep pain, students are often locked in their private misery, abandoned to their loneliness and depression.

4. Grant individual freedom according to each person's ability to discharge responsibility. Even when we failed in our responsibilities, we were willing to learn from our failures. Some children, because of their high level of consciousness, are capable of great trust, and grow tremendously by proving that they can be held accountable in difficult situations that demand good judgment. Others need to experience a series of smaller successes and failures in order to learn the value of keeping one's word and choosing ever higher standards for work and behavior.

Never esteem anything as an advantage to thee that shall makethee break thy word or lose thy self-respect.

~Marcus Aurelius [31]

5. Teach the disciplines of extended attention and focus in a variety of settings. Together, teachers and students practiced yoga, guided and unguided meditation, tai chi, aerobics, and daily fifteen minutes periods of Quiet Time. Students were encouraged to concentrate for extended periods in art, music, dance, movement, theater, and a variety of sports and other activities, as well as when studying academic subjects. For older students, most classes lasted a full hour or more. Our main intention in most classes was to help students gain inner discipline.

Quiet minds cannot be perplexed or frightened but go on in fortune or misfortune at their own private pace, like a clock during a thunderstorm.

~Robert Louis Stevenson [32]

Sustained attention, accompanied by an attitude of devotion, increases the ability for intense focus, for deep, quiet penetration, so that one is no longer separate from an object of study, but in tune with it, as in meditation. With such a discipline, an individual no longer works haphazardly; she no longer seeks diversions and interruptions, but quietly penetrates the object until she becomes one with it.

What is really important in education is not that the child learns this or that, but that the mind is matured, that energy is aroused. It doesn't make much difference what you study, as long as you don't like it.

~Soren Kierkegaard, Either/Or 6

6. Help students overcome inner resistance to life. We urged students to adopt an attitude of enthusiasm for whatever they undertook in order to foster a strong, inner acceptance of their classes and activities. We wanted students to appreciate the importance of quality work and effort, to see that by dropping resistance in any aspect of their life, more was accomplished with less effort. Their self-esteem seemed to be tied to their ability to choose a positive approach and appropriately express what they did and who they were.

Whatever necessity lays on thee, endure; whatever it commands, do.

~Johann Wolfgang Goethe 33

We were not overly anxious that students obeyed the teachers, but that they connected with their innermost potential by saying "Yes" to all the inner requirements of leading an elevated life.

Most powerful is he who has himself in his own power.

~Seneca 34

A discipline may be built whenever one attends and surrenders and falls in love with what one is doing. Discipline builds whenever one devotes oneself to an activity one loves. The choice of commitment dissolves resistance and allows the release of inner power, inner intelligence, and inner talent, as one opens and awakens to greater possibilities within a particular field. To consciously follow one's heart enlivens the inner life, causing a flow of energy and intent, which is the basis of creation.

Surrendering to a process that creates group success through individual commitment to hard work unites one with life forces. Surrender carries one over the threshold of self-consciousness and self-criticism into a space where Spirit (the ancients called these creative agents muses or gods) inspires the individual and co-creates with him. Surrender creates an inner space, a vessel, which can hold new awareness.

Power and purpose lead inevitably to the expression of Self, to joy, to fulfillment, and to a greater confidence in one's own inner resources. When education promotes this cycle of goodness and excellence, it directly serves the deepest needs of the individual and indirectly serves the greater consciousness of humanity. It can happen in music, drawing, painting, dance, theater, and in all academic subjects as well. But, according to the laws that order the universe, it cannot happen as long as a student has resistance to the very thing she is studying or doing.

Resistance occurs whenever a person self-consciously thinks about his performance, because ego thought is always engaged in defending and safeguarding one's image. So, to break through opposition is to move from ego concerns, focused on either past or future, into the present moment. Attention in the Now, without concern for how one's productions will turn out in the future, allows for full use of an inner, expanded intelligence. With focus we make use of a different, and more powerful, energy. Ego energy is temporarily suspended whenever the energy of the inner Self comes into play.

7. Provide individual challenges to students in order to encourage them to trust their ability to expand their self-image and their sense of their potential capabilities.

The short-term goal of Naked Education is to build a student's confidence in his inner resources to take bold strides down the path of his life. Confidence is gained by working from the Self while oriented in the present. It happens whenever a student makes a significant personal breakthrough of self-image and willingly and successfully takes on responsibility for something new. The breakthrough may be a new, positive attitude towards his daily job at school, taking on the responsibility of maintaining the school grounds, making a decision to sing a solo, to master drawing or dance or yoga or aerobics or meditation, choosing to shine (excel) in a school subject, or to find ease with expressing himself through writing or juggling or debating or speaking the truth. The specific nature of the change doesn't matter as long as it presents a decisive challenge and the student commits to that challenge.

A diamond with a flaw is preferable to a common stone with none.

~Chinese Proverb

After a triumph in any realm, a student knows she is excellent at something, good for something. And the community knows it as well, and respects her for it. Then, that sense of conquest or accomplishment can begin to transfer to other regions and transform them from areas of resistance to areas of positive energy. That is how a little light, step by step, becomes a powerful, penetrating beacon.

It is notorious that a single successful effort of moral volition, such as saying "no" to some habitual temptation, or performing some courageous act, will launch a man on a higher level of energy for days and weeks, will give him a new range of power.

~William James, *"The Energies of Men," Essays on Faith and Morals* [35]

8. Recognize the crucial power of individual choice in Life. Only with increased awareness comes the possibility of making new, vital decisions. There are no real choices for a personality that is controlled by the unconscious, for that ego mind is a reflexive, inflexible mind, determined by childhood conditioning of the family, the school, and the society.

Compulsive thinking prevents awareness of one's Being; thought which is unconscious has no interstices for consciousness to penetrate and flourish. Ego's non-stop, runaway thought is out-of control thinking. It is the inner equivalent of the incessant talker who spouts the same mental "tapes" without ceasing, or of the perpetual yap of a dog tied to a post (the ego). And since free choice requires a certain degree of cognizance and peace for one to see the clear consequences of distinct lines of action, it depends on consciousness, that awareness that excludes compulsive thinking. Our higher self cannot function as long as the incessant gabber holds our attention.

Life begets life. Energy creates energy. It is by spending oneself that one becomes rich.

~Sarah Bernhardt [36]

9. Encourage students to be enthusiastic about their own life and its possibilities. Enthusiasm is critical to the process of change. When a student incorporates the powerful energy of a belief in Self, he becomes connected with his full potential power, his Being. If the community, as a whole, incorporates that same energy, it is easier for the individual to jump to the next level of consciousness.

In review, our nine threads of raising consciousness were:

✓ 1. Regularly reading rich symbolic literature

✓ 2. Discussing together all aspects of our experience

✓ 3. Discussing together the paradigms of growth

✓ 4. Granting individual freedom according to one's ability to assume responsibility and concentrate

✓ 5. Teaching the disciplines of Attention and Focus in a variety of classes and settings

✓ 6. Helping students overcome Resistance to Life

✓ 7. Providing individual challenges to students

✓ 8. Using the power of Choice to create transformation

✓ 9. Encouraging students to become enthusiastic about their actual life and their life possibilities.

When these threads were woven together, the result was not only impressive, outer accomplishments, but the development of important inner qualities. A rigorous discipline develops abiding patience in the long-term process of moving ever deeper into one's work, of trusting that one will be led to ever-richer treasures.

The aim of education, in our view, is the recognition, the nourishment, and the expression of the innate intelligence (Divine life force) of each student, so that he or she develops the ability to follow an individual, personal, inner plan. To accomplish this end at The Well, students were supported by the natural process of awakening to life as a member of a community that supported the expression of Life.

As we have seen, there is much a school can do as preparation for inner development. We can prepare the garden soil; we can teach strategies and provide information about the consequences of adopting certain ideas and attitudes. But we must wait for a student's inner initiative to choose to shift his center of attention and to trust in his inner resources to make a success of it. As teachers, we had to watch and wait for individual students, one at a time, to make new choices or surrender to their higher natures. Each student does that according to his own special needs and his own, inner timetable. Often, the effect of one courageous choice becomes contagious, and inspires others to show similar courage.

In our tenure at The Well, raising awareness of a group was far easier than raising the awareness of a single individual, for a group feeds on each other's energy and enthusiasm. Although, in the long run, each individual must be able to support her own consciousness on her own, group work allows for wonderful experiences together in awareness that, in turn, can become the foundation for substantial, individual leaps in consciousness. Because awakening is facilitated through the heart center and powered by the emotions, the avenues to higher consciousness are experiences, direct and indirect, which open the heart to a greater awareness of the inner Self and the Divine nature of others. Significant encounters with life's surprises are the treasure troves of individual lives. From conscious experiences, or from unconscious experiences made conscious, come crucial realizations, direct, inner knowing, and a shift of perception. Alterations in our awareness open up new vistas for us. We call the experience of surrendering to one's higher Self, saying 'Yes' to life.

We suggest that all parents, at the moment of their child's birth, have entered, willingly or unwillingly, into a sacred contract with Life itself. In our opinion, every birth opens a door to the Divine; every parent experiences that sacred presence, revealing the unmistakable intervention of the sublime.

A central tenet of Naked Education is for a child, who is already open, to preserve that openness and embrace life fully. But for a child affected by a deadly resistance to Life, the goal is to create a habit of embracing life without fear.

Life in the present moment is the measure of a school. What, then, is the nature of Life? What distinguishes being with the power of life from being separate from it? As soon as I contemplate this question, I am reminded of the following experience that made me aware of how I, as an individual teacher, or how educational systems as collectives, can unwittingly cause the death of their students' enthusiasm for learning. The reader may also have experienced his own personal version of death via education.

In our first teaching position at Barrow, Alaska, we were given no orientation. Half an hour after our plane landed, we were greeted by the principal. We were allowed fifteen minutes to wash up. I received no instructions on my duties as a teacher or on the needs of my new students. In the hallway outside my classroom-to-be, I heard a piercing sound, which I soon recognized as a forced attempt at singing, a screeching female voice lost and wandering outside its range, searching for a harmonious note. The "song" stopped abruptly, and was replaced by simple screaming. When the principal opened the classroom door, a stout, ferocious-looking crone was delivering a tirade to the cowering class of about forty Eskimo children. She paused only a moment to acknowledge the principal and me, then with a half nod, continued her tirade.

"O.K. Who's got the rotten ear? I can smell it! It's absolutely revolting! You can't fool Backerfelt! I can always smell out a rotten ear!" Like a sergeant inspecting her troops, she walked between the rows of desks, bending with obvious difficulty as far over as she could manage while sniffing her students, one at a time. As she passed, her face twisted in a know-it-all smirk. Finally, she located and grabbed the offending ear, giving it a sharp twist for good measure. Then – for my benefit, I believe – she lectured the whole class on the need for regularly washing ears and on the stupidity of those students for ignoring her warnings about the dangers of ear infections, including the probability of the infection going directly to the brain and summarily causing death. When she had exhausted herself, she took about thirty seconds to compose herself and regain her breath, and then exited erectly and abruptly, snorting as she went.

This woman had driven the class, the principal, and me into a state of stunned silence, all eyes averted, all barely breathing. The principal recovered and beat a fast retreat, slamming the door as he went. I stood before my charges aghast. The reek of death permeated the air. I was now to commit my first action as a representative of the United States Bureau of Indian Affairs. Somehow, deep down, I understood I was working in an official capacity for Death (the spiritual death of the Native American). This was the first of my many lessons as a fledgling teacher, noting what was inimical to the life of students. As a student, the experience already had proved too familiar.

I prayed that somehow I might learn to bring life and hope and possibility to my students.

As a student in my youth, I had noticed that kids are much more alive outside the classroom than inside it. Outside, they can let down, breathe deeply, and laugh. The typical educational paradigm, it seems, defies Life by building artificial walls that separate vital activities outside school from a cloistered prison-like staleness inside. For the most part, schools intentionally separate professional teachers, authorities in the know, from their students. Teachers are trained not to communicate anything personal or intimate with their students. It might create the impression of equality with their underlings and threaten their outer authority. How would they then control their students? Control in some systems is seen as the key!

We believe it is wrongly assumed that teachers know and students are ignorant, that genuine authority is a natural result of advanced consciousness, and that the need to control other human beings is an unworthy sign of an extremely limited consciousness.

My own childhood educational experience relied more on ingesting "objective" facts, and taking "objective" tests to determine "scientifically" how effectively the transfer of information from teacher to student had occurred. Teaching was assumed to be a direct, one-way current, flowing from teacher to child. Because this authoritarian paradigm assumes that the child is deficient and needs the teacher to first provide, and then check, the answers, it introduces a co-dependent, negative relationship between teacher and student in which students who know comply out of fear of the authorities with school expectations and automatically defer to teachers, even if they know the teacher is in error. Provide the child with enough teachers, enough fear-based co-dependent relationships, and he will eventually possess a modicum of memorized information. But throughout this process, the student will remain ignorant of himself and his inner treasure of Being. His potential wisdom will lie buried within. Such is the hypocrisy of an "education" which fails to draw forth the inner wealth of each student.

We're in a free fall into the future. We don't know where we're going. Things are changing so fast. And always when you're going through a long tunnel, anxiety comes along. But all you have to do to transform your hell into a paradise is to turn your fall into a voluntary act. It's a very interesting shift of perspective. Joyfully participate in the sorrows of the world and everything changes."

~Joseph Campbell, *Sukhavati*

When one assumes that teacher and children are connected to the source of Life, the source of knowledge, and possess, deep within them, a map for their own life, education takes on a different purpose and follows an alternate course (the metaphor is alternating current instead of direct current). Then the teacher must work with the instincts and talents of the student as a given, vital resource and take direction from each individual, as well as from his own personal depths. There are no external lesson plans that accomplish this. Teacher and students must create the lesson together. The student-teacher relationship becomes a living partnership of two creative beings, each of infinite value, forging a joint experience that nourishes both.

The authentic teacher who makes a conscious commitment to see the potential and the greatness in a child decides to ever hold that child in the light of love, however he behaves. On that basis, a teacher will reveal (rather than conceal) her Being, and share a significant portion of her life journey with the parallel journey of her students. The classroom comes alive through interchanges between equal beings. Little "miracles" become the norm.

Ah, but a man's reach should exceed his grasp, or what is heaven for?

~Andrea del Sarto [37]

These platitudes express The Well School experience of Naked Education: "Nothing can stop a positive attitude! Enthusiasm carries the day! Gratitude provides the impetus for transformation! Love dissolves all barriers!"

Naked Education involves honest communication and real life challenges, a living dialogue between Beings about the ongoing nature of human life and the truth of inexhaustible and unlimited human potential. Naked Education is a spontaneous dance in the moment, dignified and artful, expressive of the current reality.

Notes:

NOTES:

CHAPTER 3: THE ROLE OF DRAMA

My candle burns at both ends;
It will not last the night;
But ah, my foes, and oh, my friends
It gives a lovely light.

~Edna St. Vincent Millay [1]

Let me describe a few typical snapshots of the joy I encountered while teaching at The Well School. These pictures are intended to portray the culture that lay behind our play productions, a culture that stressed making a commitment and surrendering in advance to a process; visualizing a great success; exercising great discipline, responsibility, and self-reliance and striving to do justice to a great work of art. In our presentation, we will discuss many aspects of productions of Shakespeare's *Twelfth Night* and Leonard Bernstein's *West Side Story,* and will include clips of the history of drama at The Well School. We will also take a few shots of the larger culture of The Well, which supported our theatrical subculture.

Twelfth Night:

Picture a turned-on student: friendly and open with classmates and adults, energetic yet at ease, excited by the promise of each day, obviously smart, responsive, articulate, concerned about the welfare of others, a team-player in situations which require cooperation, and a self-motivator in terms of his own projects.

Now, picture ten of these students with the same basic qualities in a class: examining the patterns of Fibonacci numbers, creating a 19th century village in miniature, reading in Latin the story of a con-artist, discussing Alex Haley's *Roots*, drawing a still life of a pair of sneakers, reading their own poetry aloud to each other, learning about grammar, playing basketball during a break from a grammar lesson, meditating, learning martial arts, experimenting with the physics of bouncing balls, writing an essay, eating lunch, moving a pile of wood, or practicing a recorder piece. It really doesn't matter what they are doing. What matters is that they're on fire, turned on, eager to come to school, enthusiastic about what each day holds for them.

Now picture four classes (grades 5–8) of these students rehearsing for a production of Shakespeare's *Twelfth Night*. In a 40' x 40' room, 21 kids are doing homework seated at four rectangular, folding tables. In time, they will all rehearse their scenes. Five on stage are practicing the scene where the officious steward, Malvolio, rebukes Sir Toby Belch, Sir Andrew Aguecheek, and the Jester – while a mischievous servant, Maria, listens with delight just offstage – for singing off key at the top of their voices in the middle of the night, daring to awaken Olivia, the lady of the house. The doubles of these five characters, those who will perform on alternate nights (most parts are double-cast), watch and learn. They will have their turn rehearsing in a few minutes. One who has missed the last two rehearsals is being coached by his double.

Meanwhile, five others are working together as a team, four setting the lights with ladders and a hydraulic lift, one commanding the lighting board, turning lights off and on as needed.

Where are the other four? They have slipped off to the kitchen of our house and are readying a dinner made up of portions that each of them has brought from home, a dinner of macaroni and cheese, chicken wings, salad, milk, and Oreo cookies. They are laying out the silverware and lighting dozens of candles in four classrooms, which are also part of our house.

As is often the case, there is only one adult present to supervise these 40 children, and I cannot split myself to be in both buildings in order to oversee and patrol what is happening. That's OK. I'm enjoying our interpretation of this very funny scene. I am shouting out, "Let's take it from Malvolio's entrance. Toby, Andrew, Feste, you've got to sing more off key, louder, and Malvolio, your character is not so pleasant; he has lost all control of himself, so you need to be especially outrageous.

We began our 11th rehearsal at 3:45 and will end at 8:15, when the parents arrive to pick up the kids. From 6:00 to 6:30, we will all eat our supper together. Toni will join me after dinner to direct for a while, giving suggestions, and allowing me to relax and take a break. This is our sixth week of rehearsal. In another three weeks, we'll put on four productions for the community. We're excited.

How does it happen that kids aged 10 to 14, with relatively little supervision, can memorize and understand, depending on their role, 20 to 500 lines of Shakespeare, focus on homework in a three-ring-circus kind of environment, competently set the lighting 18 feet above the stage, learn to use and program a professional lighting board, efficiently and tastefully prepare a dinner so as to enjoy the meal together, fool around, vacuum the rugs, clean the tables, wash the dishes, and have the energy to play a little basketball before resuming rehearsal at 6:45? Why do the great majority of kids choose to do this after six challenging hours of class earlier in the day? Why do they behave and look after one another? Why are they acting, for the most part, like mature, motivated adults?

There are so many answers. One is that many have already performed in two or three Shakespeare productions. That helps a lot. Another answer is that they believe they are capable of doing almost anything well because they have done a thousand things well already. Another is that the three or four poems students publicly recite at the school each year give them extra confidence speaking and standing before a group of parent, teachers, and peers. And our high expectations, I believe, also support them in their striving for greatness.

And there are more reasons why the process of dramatic production works. The actors know that if problems arise (as they always do), we will stop what we are doing and talk about our goal of putting on a great play, and the requirement that everyone monitors his own behavior and plays his part well for it to work. Sometimes, there is a need to choose again. (Do you really want this part? You have a double who can step in and take your place. If you choose to stay, you must be willing to pay the price.) The price is time, focus, self-motivation, energy, commitment, and enthusiasm. It's the same price paid by all students and teachers at The Well.

Such intense enthusiasm is mirrored by this Emily Dickinson poem:

> *I taste a liquor never brewed –*
> *From Tankards scooped in pearl –*
> *Not all the vats upon the Rhine*
> *Yield such an Alcohol!*
> *Inebriate of air – am I –*
> *And Debauchee of Dew,*
> *Reeling – thro endless summer days –*
> *From inns of molten Blue*
> *When "Landlords" turn the drunken Bee*
> *Out of the Foxglove's door –*
> *When Butterflies – renounce their "drams" –*
> *I shall but drink the more!*
> *Till seraphs swing their snowy Hats,*
> *And Saints to windows run -*
> *To see the little Tippler*
> *Leaning against the – Sun.*

~Emily Dickinson [2]

And there is a further reason. By The Well's second year of existence, it already had a distinctive culture and tradition of its own that included ideas like:

♪ Everybody Does Everything

♪ Always Do Your Best

♪ Expect Great Things to Happen

♪ Let Everyone Join In

♪ Focus is Power

♪ Excel at Academics, as well as the Arts

♪ Sing Your Heart Out at Chorus

♪ We All Move and Stack the Wood that Heats the Classrooms

♪ Make Your Own Lunch at home

♪ Gratitude is the Best Attitude

♪ Use Your Voice and Contribute to exchanges at Meetings

♪ We All Play Eskimo Baseball

♪ We All Clean the Barn, Shovel the Snow

♪ Do Your Job After School with Gusto

♪ Take Responsibility for Yourself

♪ Love What You Do

♪ Do Something Special for Your Parents Every Day

♪ You May Express your Greatness in many Areas

♪ Clap for Everyone

♪ Expect the Best; Have Faith in Yourself

♪ Love is a Choice

Kids actually love to do and do and do. When they are flagging, they need a little supervision or inspiration; they need to know that others care and are working hard, too.

Often, when new students who were non-movers in a number of departments entered our school, they adjusted like magic to the prevailing culture, and caught up to the others so that they might swim effortlessly with the other "fish in the sea."

First graders see their 13-year-old friend, Mark, singing, *"I Want Money"* in a student production of *The Taming of the Shrew* with 15 hot Beatles tunes (the older kids were the ones who found the music to fit the play during a Project Month class). Younger siblings showed up three nights in a row to see the play and watch their sibling, Mary, sing *"It's a Hard Day's Night"* (they often sit on the floor in front of the stage, only three feet away from the nearest actors). By now, they understand much of Shakespeare without knowing it (the action is not that hard to follow), and dream of having their turn some day, of having as much fun as Mary has when she isn't Mary at all, but Katherine expressing her rage. Younger students, especially those with older brothers and sisters, feed into, strengthen, and enliven the existing culture with their own enthusiasm because they anticipate doing the same play in a few years.

Better yet, when the older students need the younger ones as fairies for *A Midsummer Night's Dream*, or cherubs in heaven for Marc Connelly's *Green Pastures*, they share the thrill of being on stage with much older kids and help generate the energy of the show.

> *I think the young actor who really wants to act will find a way – There's no advice you can really offer except to keep at it and seize every opportunity that comes along.*
>
> ~Sir John Gielgud, *Showcase by Roy Newquist* [3]

Notice that the dynamic of putting on a play breaks the mold of everyone doing the same assignment, doing the same work, and introduces different expectations for different people according to their experience, abilities, and interests. The various roles are not artificially assigned (that would be Death!), but closely correspond to the wishes of the students. They declare in advance of any commitment how large a part they want, and which parts and which choreography and music they are interested in, including the technical support roles dealing with lighting, sound, sets, and props.

Someone has to make the final decisions. One aspect of casting was always very enjoyable, because I could see in advance the shape this production could take and sense the energy potential for each scene. But casting, for me, was also the most burdensome stage of production. Although most students received the parts they volunteered for, there were usually some disappointments, and occasionally a broken heart that needed healing. I felt so responsible for each disappointment, for each crushed heart, that I was sometimes less than gracious in dealing with the fallout, which could be overwhelming for me as well.

From my point of view, Naked Education always presents challenges, moving students from where they are to a higher level of functioning. The kid with 20 lines might need help with clear enunciation, voice projection, or keeping her head up so an audience could see her face. Or the child with 100 lines might need help with moving on stage and expressing the character's emotions. And the children with more lines, those who are most relaxed in front of an audience (perhaps they've already been in a dozen plays) and totally into their parts, need several rehearsals where the interruptions are minimal so they can learn to feel and regulate the pace of each scene.

In the excitement of a performance, these leaders will slow the action so each word can be heard, so there is time for the characters to react to each other, and for the actors to reveal their characters instead of just saying their lines. Real drama, from my point of view, occurs in the pauses before lines, within lines, or between lines, when actors look at or away from each other.

The thrill of drama, for me, is transmitting living archetypes embedded in a play to the audience by making them accessible and immediate, palpable and real.

As a director I never tired or lost patience as long as my energy was devoted to refining a scene. That effort required the synthesis of all the forces at work: the understanding of the actors, their interplay with each other, the placement of the actors on stage, the lighting, the sound, the use of props, the scenery. When everything worked to the same end, I was sustained and enlivened by the process. When focus was broken, I felt, for a moment, as if I were broken.

The composer Stravinsky had written a new piece with a difficult violin passage. After it had been in rehearsal for several weeks, the solo violinist came to Stravinsky and said he was sorry, he had tried his best, the passage was too difficult, no violinist could play it. Stravinsky said, "I understand that. What I am after is the sound of someone trying to play it."

~Thomas Powers [4]

West Side Story:

I would like to include some details of putting on West Side Story, including how our extraordinary dance program played into it, to indicate how consuming the process could be, how deeply the project depended on the focused energy of students, former students, teachers, former teachers, parents, former parents, and friends of the school. This hearts-on learning brought out the extraordinary talents of every child in four grade levels, because all those talents were desperately needed.

There was no busy work for the sake of a modicum of learning. All the effort, all the learning coalesced around a great work of art, in this case *West Side Story*, a brilliant modern take on Shakespeare's classic *Romeo and Juliet*, heightened by some of the most expressive and compelling examples of modern composition by the great Leonard Bernstein (once himself a regular summer frequenter of our town of Peterborough, New Hampshire). To me, the best served to inspire our best.

Ode to a Grecian Urn

> *O Attic shape! Fair attitude! with brede*
> *Of marble men and maidens overwrought,*
> *With forest branches and the trodden weed;*
> *Thou, silent form, dost tease us out of thought*
> *As doth eternity; Cold pastoral!*
>
> *When old age shall this generation waste,*
> *Thou shalt remain, in midst of other woe*
> *Than ours, a friend to man, to whom thou say'st,*
> *Beauty is truth, truth beauty, – that is all*
> *Ye know on earth, and all ye need to know.*

~John Keats [5]

The best art inspires great art. It is the classical form of education, that both honors truth and beauty, and then challenges us to emulate it. *West Side Story* initiated our third performance space, the first dedicated theater on campus.

> *The aesthetic sense is very close to the religious; beauty has a great educative power.*
>
> ~Alexis Carrel, *Reflections of Life* [6]

> *The contemplation of truth and beauty is a proper object for which we were created, which calls forth the most intense desires of the soul, and of which it never tires.*
>
> ~William Hazlitt, *Criticism of Art* [7]

West Side Story presented a special challenge because it would be our first production in an entirely new performance space, the first dedicated theater on campus. It forced the actors to adapt to a stage much larger than the one where they rehearsed, and play to a much larger audience.

Our first theater space was generously provided by one of the original Well families, the Eldredges. They volunteered their huge, rustic studio room, which ordinarily served as their living room. (Occasionally, they hosted jazz concerts there as well, for the room could hold over 200 people!) Since the shortest way from The Well to the Eldredge's was a bee line through the woods, the kids cut a trail with Swiss saws, axes, and clippers – nobody would get lost traveling to and from rehearsals – that enabled us to make the trek in thirty minutes. Although an hour was added to each rehearsal, nobody seemed to mind, for it allowed a time for hooting, skipping along, and spontaneous conversation as we passed through the beautiful woods, which always seemed a sacred place.

The second theater was a 24' x 56' two-level classroom heated largely by wood. The labor it took for the kids and me to transform the classroom into a theater and back again was excessive, but this space served our purposes for many years and cut out the time of the trek through the woods., Liz Verney, our art teacher and parent who taught at The Well, however, was shocked at the effort required to transform the room, and led a group of parents to build a new arts wing onto our library building. We were deeply appreciative.

When the work was almost completed on the new wing, the building inspector seemed to go out of his way to create as many obstacles as possible to opening the building in time for our performances. The two builders, a former parent, Rob, and another carpenter, Bub, had waited for over a month to get approval from the town of Peterborough to occupy the building. As our school year neared its end, they sealed off the theater from the rest of the building in hopes of getting just the theater approved. The plan was to have everyone enter through the emergency exits – no going to the bathroom once we began – it's off limits. We did have a contingency plan of using the neighboring professional stage of the Peterborough Players (years before, we had used it to put on a performance of *A Midsummer Night's Dream*, but these children had never practiced in that space, and there was no lighting set up.

Our inspector approved the theater for occupancy late in the afternoon two days before the first of our productions of *West Side Story*, although the entire new wing had not been approved. Anticipating that the building inspector would sympathize with our great need, a parent, Charlie, and I had hung the lights in the simplest of patterns the night before the show. Fortunately, the cast had twice before illegally invaded the theater space to see how the acting and dancing worked in the new stage area. None of us had any idea of what would happen if our new theater could not be used; we refused to consider it an option.

To drive home the point that we relied on great optimism (or was it miracles?) for the functioning of our school, let me tell you about the dancing aspect of the show. In *West Side Story*, the impact of the show requires fine, energetic, almost frenetic dancing. Yes, the "Jets' Song," "Gee, Officer Krupke," and "I Feel Pretty" needed choreography. But the Sharks' "America," a mambo dance which takes place on a gang's New York City rooftop, requires what I can only call a fancy, show-off style, where boys and girls take turns trying to outdo each other in their stylish movements, then synchronize together as one group, before returning to more competitive sections. It is a tall order to imitate the flamboyant style and pride of these Puerto Rican teenagers. Then, there's the Jet's dance "Cool," which takes place in an abandoned garage, after a rumble with the Sharks has left Riff, the spiritual leader of the Jets, dead. The dance must be dramatic and, well, "cool," building to a wild, desperate crescendo to match the desperation experienced by the Jets. The Jets having lost their confidence, their cool, regain it through their macho dance in the garage.

Putting on this play was, at first, unthinkable, even for students who love a challenge. But during the year that the theater was being built, a new Well School student in eighth grade, and an old Well School student in eighth grade, were so outstanding in their dancing that all bets were off. They were chosen as lead dancers for the New Hampshire Dance Institute, a program for 250 children which culminates near the end of each year in four performances at Keene State College's Brickyard Pond in Keene, New Hampshire.

The NHDI program dares ordinary kids to be outrageously disciplined and artistically expressive in their approach to dance. Jacques D'Amboise, who came to the conclusion that dance had saved his own life, founded the National Dance Institute in 1976 after a career as a principal dancer in the New York City Ballet. His purpose was to get kids into artistic dancing and to remove them from the temptations and violence of the streets of New York City.

Wendy Dwyer, a dancer and choreographer whose child attended The Well, created a New Hampshire satellite, NHDI, and had been artistic director of the program since its inception. Our school, under Wendy's direction for many years, was one of nine to twelve schools participating in the program.

Each year, NHDI has a different theme and much original music, and employs a formula: each school does two dances of its own, and then all the schools join together for the finales to both Act I and Act II, all 250 children dancing together on one stage. But Wendy also selected a "SWAT" team of the most outstanding dancers in the program from all the participating schools who, in addition to their school dances, worked three hours every Saturday at a central meeting place to create more challenging dances which, when incorporated into the larger program, inspired everyone in the regular program to dance their feet off.

Our Charlie and Greg, leading members of the NHDI SWAT team, were up for *West Side Story*. When we couldn't find a choreographer, they said they thought they could do the choreography. They watched videos of *West Side Story* and decided, with a few simplifications of steps, they could teach everybody the dances. Provisionally, we decided to go ahead. Charlie would play the lead Shark, Bernardo, and Greg the lead Jet, Riff.

The first dance rehearsal provided an acid test. Sure enough, Greg and Charlie had learned the dance, and even the boys with two left feet were following their lead, enlivened by the two spirited exemplars and the spell of *West Side Story*. Several girls proved talented in picking up the steps for the other girls and executing them with flair. Two had extensive dance training (ballet, as well as several other dance forms) as part of larger dance troupes. *West Side Story* provided a golden opportunity for them to demonstrate their mettle as lead dancers. Other girls got to show off the high kicks they achieved from years of aerobics at our school.

We also engaged the services of amateur dance teachers, Toni, and her teacher/sidekick at the time, Pam Nation, whose uninhibited demonstrations of dancing broke the ice with the kids. Their responsibility was the high school dance, which takes place just before the Jets and the Sharks challenge each other to a rumble. So a couple of hours per week, we practiced a swing number and a mambo dance to the same music that would be used in the show. Although partnering couples of this age can be a nightmare, these actors had a great excuse to relax and enjoy: it's only a musical. Those couples so inclined learned fancy dancing after the regular class. Showing off was important to the plot, but those who found it daring enough just to follow the regular steps concentrated all their attention on the basics.

The show was dynamite! The costumes were created by Betsy Odgers – our first-grade teacher – who had a great sense of beauty and flair, with the help of a host of teachers and parents. The set was quickly constructed by a team of parents and students led by Liz Verney, one of our art instructors, and Charlie Massin, a school parent. It included a cut-off car that Charlie had picked up from the junkyard in his hometown, and which we had electrified to light the garage for "Cool."

About 60 lighting changes were controlled by a parent, Charlie Briggs, because we did not have an opportunity to get the kids involved in lighting before the room was approved.

The scenery painted on the large wall behind the stage was a semi-abstract mural of a section of a New York City neighborhood executed in two days by teachers, parents, and former students.

An especially talented band was put together by a parent, Tom Pucciarello, a skillful drummer. The band included a friend of the school, Frank Fiske, on synthesizer, and a musician friend of Tom's who played electric guitar.

In our new space, we needed a rehearsal to learn to balance, through the soundboard, the level of the kids' microphones with the volume of the band. (During performances, nevertheless, there were a few moments of awful feedback as we learned to deal with the sound levels of various microphones.) Some of the music was recorded, because the kids had learned one dance to a CD of the show, and another to a video recording of *West Side Story*, and they had to match their footwork exactly to that music.

And then there were the brilliant actors whose performances and energy levels reflected their dedication and trust in the process. We had magically consecrated our new building with the energy of hundreds.

Production before any audience creates intense, accelerated learning, and an energy high. While the stimulation is exhilarating, I must confess to being exhausted before and after productions, sometimes to the point of wanting to throw in the towel. When my body had run out of reserves, I often needed to turn to the kids, explain my frustration, and ask for help. As our art teacher, Kate, once said while she was working on scenery during a rehearsal, "Let's make Jay lie down and all together we'll all surround him and give him a massage. If we can revive Jay, we can put on the play." It worked for me and for everybody else.

Over the years I did learn to ask for more and more help from my students and take less of the burden on myself. If truth be spoken, these students had already surpassed me in so many ways. In my only acting experience in eighth grade, I spewed out a few words while ironing a dress shirt in a 15-minute school play marking Veterans Day. And in my other teaching duties – typically five, hour-long classes each day – there always had been students ahead of me in one field of activity or another: in speed reading; in getting the details of a reading selection right in English literature, in Ancient and American History studies, in spelling, in finding editing mistakes, in quickness in math, in learning Spanish or Latin, and, of course, in using any computer program.

> *It did not insult my intelligence to have students surpass me; in fact, it only motivated students to be able to correct a teacher and have the teacher agree that the student was right, and the teacher was wrong."*
>
> ~Jay Garland [8]

Although I doubted my own ability to do what so many of our young actors were doing, to memorize and take on large roles, I never doubted my ability to direct others who lacked that same confidence. I knew the secret of my own success as a director: choose a great play, preferably full-length; decide in advance that the play will be exceptional, and let each child's intuition suggest which parts he or she wants to play. Then, without pre-planning, read the lines with the cast and ask questions, make comments. Do the same again while the actors stand on stage. Follow any intuitive urges.

My underlying intent was for the actors to completely identify with their roles, and to follow their creative interpretations in terms of acting. Often, their ideas were superior to my own, and we would adopt them. If that strategy failed to produce a character with energy, I would interrupt and play the part myself until the actor appreciated the level of energy required. This short demonstration tended to inspire the individual to apply the same energy to his whole part. If a scene failed to live, I would interrupt to say, "That doesn't work! We have to come up with something better." And we'd discuss what it might be, and try different ideas for staging the scene until it worked.

When all the scenes seemed effective, we just ran through the play as much as possible to gain confidence. If we were stuck, standing still, or regressing, I called a meeting to decide – together with the cast – whether to cancel the play or come up with a new plan to be properly prepared. At that point, the kids always had the will to rally, to re-commit.

To me, group performance begins with a vision of what is possible, a clear purpose. Its success depends on convincing the participants to make a definite choice: to commit to every stage of the process, by suspending their doubts and anxieties and surrendering to each step of the way. Making a clear-cut choice frees one and releases the energy and will to follow the process through to the end. There are always bumps along the way – times of discouragement – but as the work unfolds, and each individual notices his own transformation as well as the transformations of others, the group energy and confidence builds to a grand crescendo. Each learns that by depending on her own innate resources to play her part, she can discover and express more than she ever considered possible, and become part of something larger than herself. For me, success in such a project is measured by whether each individual's self-image is enlarged and enhanced in the end, whether her trust in her own potential grows.

Our attempts at dramatic success were simply a scene in miniature of what it takes to be successful in life: a vision, commitment, teamwork, and responsible execution. The greater the assent the greater the success:

> *I'll not confer with sorrow till tomorrow;*
> *But joy shall have her way, this very day.*
> *Tears, if you will, but after mirth and laughter;*
> *Then folded hands on breast and endless rest!*

~Thomas Bailey Aldrech [9]

NOTES:

NOTES:

CHAPTER 4: THE LOSS OF CONSCIOUSNESS IN SCHOOLS

Iron rusts from disuse, stagnant water loses its purity and in cold weather becomes frozen; even so does inaction shape the vigor of the mind.

~Leonardo Da Vinci [1]

As founders of The Well School in 1967, Toni and I were very aware that our primary focus was to raise the consciousness of ourselves and those associated with the school. After the first five years of directing The Well School, we became more convinced of the practical utility and moral necessity of not only facilitating consciousness, but also of becoming more conscious ourselves.

Men have now arrived at such a high pitch of civilization that all institutions which act in any way to obstruct or thwart the development of the individual, and compress men together into vast uniform masses, are now far more hurtful than in earlier ages of the world.

~Alexander von Humboldt, *The Sphere and Duty of Government* [2]

During the years from 1972 to 2002, we often observed that while we were seeking to expand the consciousness of The Well School community, education in the rest of the country was proceeding in the opposite direction, building walls against awareness.

The trend across the United States was to build larger schools. In the early days of The Well, in the late 1960s and the early 1970s, the federal government was offering to pay the lion's share of the construction of new, larger consolidated schools that replaced schools that primarily served single towns. For many years, there had been a national movement by politicians and educational specialists to create insulated educational systems that removed any control of education from parents and gave it to educational bureaucrats, consultants, administrators, and politicians. Today, that process is complete.

If we look back at the history of education in our country from the time of the founding until the present, what is apparent is that we have had only three clearly differentiated periods of U.S. education.

1. *The Era of Voluntary Education*
   Parents could decide the kind of education they desired for their children. Education was dominated by home schooling. Most people learned to read at home, and even those who were extremely well educated had less than three years of formal instruction, mostly at private schools, and mostly for three or four hours a day, 30 to 90 days a year.

   The common schools in New England taught the Calvinist Puritan doctrines. The Puritans intentionally modeled these schools after those created by Martin Luther. In addition, there were specialized private schools that prepared students for society life, college, or religious studies.

2. *The Era of Transition to Compulsory Education*
   Over a period of 67 years (from 1852 to 1918), one state after another was persuaded to adopt compulsory education laws and penalties for truancy, along with child labor laws. State by state, over the years, control over the child was effectively transferred from the parents to the state school systems.

3. *The Era of Compulsory Education*
   The first state compulsory education was created by a highly respected Massachusetts lawyer, state representative, and senator, Horace Mann. His own schooling consisted of not more than six weeks per year during his teens, but Horace Mann, a legislator and later the first Secretary of Education in Massachusetts, was destined to fall under the spell of the rigidly ordered Prussian school movement. On his summer honeymoon tour to Germany in 1843 (while schools were on vacation), he briefly visited a Prussian compulsory school and was persuaded by a few conversations to import the entire Prussian system to America, despite the fact that he never viewed a Prussian school in operation.

Mann coveted order, and having been frustrated in trying to standardize Massachusetts's schools, saw the already completed Prussian model as a shortcut to his goal. His success in adopting Prussian-style schools changed the course not only of

American education, but of American history as well.

For Mann imported a cynical system created by elite Prussian industrialists at the onset of the Industrial Revolution in order to produce a fascist state with an ideology that promoted:

♯ Dictatorial government

♯ Centralized control of the national economy, political decisions, military life and operations, and education

♯ Stiff and violent repression of any opposition or variance in ideas

♯ Censorship of artistic expression

♯ Record keeping and regular surveillance of its citizens

♯ Unquestioned nationalism.

Prussia's highest virtue was absolute obedience to authority. For this small group of industrialists, the goal was generating the highest profits possible in a state that sponsored an invincible army. There were, in short, no individual rights or liberties, except for the elite. All power was held by the state, and controlled by the industrialists.

Prussia's educational system, which Mann investigated, was two-faced. For the elite the Realschule was to be the place where true education would take place. Here, students would freely interact, discuss topics, debate and, in general, learn to think. Here they would gain leadership skills and become identified with the elite class. Here they would dabble in classical education. Horace Mann, however, rejected this system of education in favor of one that specialized in creating robots for factories and the military.

According to John Gatto's highly documented *Underground History of American Education*, 92% of Prussian children were forced to attend the school that prepared students for one of two occupations: obedient service as soldiers in the army, or obedient workers in the factories.

This school for commoners was the Volksschule. It was this model that Horace Mann chose to adopt and transplant to Massachusetts, this model that was to be eventually adopted by every state in the United States, and then by our federal government, and which has become in everything but name our federal system of compulsory, national education. Everything in this school was designed to break the spirit of individuals and to train them to become bored, undifferentiated sheep, willing to sacrifice individuality for the glory of the state.

Prussia, as the first military-industrial-educational complex to inaugurate the Industrial

Revolution, appealed to industrialists in America and throughout the world. Because Prussia represented the triumph of fascist planning and practice, it inspired the would-be fascist industrialists everywhere, as did Hitler's absolutist beliefs and propaganda in a later age. It maximized and guaranteed obscene profits for the already wealthy. It created an army of compliant, submissive workers for industry and a military force capable of defeating Napoleon at Waterloo in 1815, and exacting revenge on France for humiliating Prussia in the battle of Jena in 1806. It proved to the satisfaction of many that "might makes right," that to the brutal victor come all the spoils.

Prussia's unrivaled military and economic success was the model for new corporations around the world to inspect the basics of mass production and then emulate the new Prussian system back home. Then new great corporations from around the world raped the world's resources, employing national armies to secure obscene profits. Unskilled workers in their assembly-line factories earned pitiful wages, creating a new super-wealthy class. The Industrial Revolution was in full bloom by the 1940s. The madness of the middle and late 19th century mass production became the insanity of corporate greed, advocating consumerism, and demanding conformity and strict obedience of it employees.

The new Prussian system of compulsory education rounded up Prussians living in the countryside and forced them to move to cities and involuntarily attend schools that stripped away individual freedoms in order to promote unthinking conformity was also copied in many advanced countries around the world.

In our educational system today, we are judged by how well we conform to the system. Students are only recognized as egos who perform tasks set before them, egos with a reputation for being smart or dumb, egos with a track record of successes or failures reflected by a record of their grades. Our report cards reflect in a single, simple grade our ego accomplishments and ego humiliations in a system of competition.

~John Gatto, *The Underground History of American Education* [21]

In today's schools our inner Being does not matter, our inner wisdom and intuition are ignored. Our kindness and compassion are overlooked. Our inner essence does not exist in today's schools. Our spiritual Being leaves no traces.

Once a student leaves school, his new report card is the amount of money he makes. We are defined by our jobs and by our pay.

~John Gatto, *The Underground History of American Education* [21]

In the 1840s, the totalitarian state of Prussia adopted many strategies reminiscent of the first state educational system of the ancient military camp of Sparta. Those strategies, which clearly reveal the mindset of its proponents, included:

1. Compulsory attendance

2. Regimentation and uniformity and standardization in all aspects of the school day

3. Worship of efficiency and mechanization

4. Centralized control of all schools

5. Planned limited intellectual development

6. Socially Engineered Obedience and Subordination – managing the thought life of children through the new Scientific Psychology of Mind Control and Conditioned Learning

7. Science at the center of the curriculum

8. Universal Standards for all children

9. State controlled Teacher Certification

10. Segregating children in classrooms by age

11. Universal Child Labor Laws preventing students from working (competing with the industrialists as entrepreneurs)

12. Indoctrination with a rigid, planned curriculum for all grades

13. Forbidding the use of phonics in learning to read

14. Use of Controlled Vocabulary to regulate what students could read and could not read

15. Reliance on State Sponsored Textbooks (information was homogenized, altered, made politically correct, passionless – dull)

16. Social studies – with pointed lessons on how to be an ideal citizen – replaced any knowledge of history and the historical process

17. The use of the bogus science of Phrenology (bumps on the head represent developed and undeveloped regions of the brain) to manage student behavior

18. The state, not the parents, is the "loving parent and legal protector of each child"

Prussian schools thus foreshadowed the employment of compulsory schooling for indoctrination in the Democratic/Republican United States, in Great Britain, in Soviet Russia, in Fascist Italy, in Nazi Germany, and Imperial Japan.

Prussia, it is clear, was a state where absolute control could not even be questioned. This repressive regime totally managed the life of its citizens. The surveillance of the state reached into every aspect of life. In this way, the system would guarantee education of the state, by the state, and for the state. The child became the moldable property of the state, to be used solely for its purposes.

All 18 of these strategies of fascist Prussia were seized on by Horace Mann and made part of the Massachusetts public schools; most were in place within a decade. There were many in Massachusetts, – probably the majority – that could not reconcile individual liberty with compulsory, state-sponsored education, and who strongly resisted turning their children over to the state.

But Mann was a powerful individual with a network of strong political connections gained by his years as a Massachusetts representative and senator. He was known for being a persuasive orator, a successful lawyer, for his office as President of the Massachusetts' Senate, for his aggressive establishing of educational reforms and forceful attempts to standardize and regulate schools as secretary of the Massachusetts Board of Education, and for creating a well-regulated Massachusetts lunatic asylum in Worcester. Everyone who owed him a favor was enlisted to vote or persuaded others to vote for his compulsory school bill. The law passed in Massachusetts in 1852. The Prussian model of education had been successfully transplanted to America! From that point on, America was destined to be controlled in its entirety by the industrial magnates.

Mann was able to introduce an officially non-sectarian education that, in fact, was based on good Protestant principles that would protect the state from the huge influx of Catholics from Ireland.

Over the next seventy years, battles between proponents of a free educational system (mostly parents) and those who advocated the uniformity that could only be accomplished through compulsory education, a la Prussia, would be waged in every other state as well. The combination of political power and the interests of business eventually overcame the unorganized opposition of parents, although 16 states resisted and opposed the process until early in the 20th century.

The pace of other states mimicking Massachusetts was slow, but relentless. Not until fifteen years after the historic decision by Massachusetts did another state, Vermont, endorse compulsory education (1867).

In the 1870s, 13 more states joined the movement: New Hampshire, Michigan, and Washington (1871); Connecticut (1872); Nevada (1873); California, Kansas, and New York (1874); Maine and New Jersey (1875); Wyoming (1876); Ohio (1877); Wisconsin (1879).

In the next decade, ten states adopted compulsory schooling: Illinois, Montana, North Dakota, South Dakota, Rhode Island (the last of the northeastern states) (1883); Minnesota (1885); Idaho and Nebraska (1887); and Colorado and Oregon (1889).

In the 1890s, another eight states voted for compulsory education: Utah (1890); New Mexico (1891); Pennsylvania (1895); Hawaii (then a territory) and Kentucky (1896); Indiana and West Virginia (1897); and Arizona (1899).

In the first decade of the 20th century, nine more states succumbed: Iowa and Maryland (1902); Missouri and Tennessee (1905); Delaware, North Carolina, and Oklahoma (1907); Virginia (1908); and Arkansas (1909).

Seven more states joined the ranks and capitulated in the next decade, all from the South: Louisiana (1910); Alabama, South Carolina, Florida, and Texas (1915); Georgia (1916); Mississippi (1918).

The territory of Alaska didn't fall in line until 1929.

After their capitulation, individual states used their discretion on how strictly to compel their students to accept the formula based on authoritarian absolutism.

For me, as a student in the compulsory education system (grades K–12), as a teacher working for the paternalistic Bureau of Indian Affairs' government schools in Inuit (Eskimo) communities in Alaska (I had to leave because the politics of the bureau tore my heart out), as a teacher in a typical private school (I rebelled at the lack of individual expression and the extreme control exercised on the student body), and as a founder of The Well School, compulsory education was repulsive. We refuted the fascistic model and the thinking that inevitably supports it and created, instead, an education devoted to the development of individual consciousness, individual expression, and the knowledge that comes from honoring individual experience.

The irony is that the great majority of teachers working in our national, compulsory, education system are well-meaning individuals, some deeply committed to the welfare of their students, as well as to the obligatory requirements of their job. This irony is compounded by another irony: the vast, American public is almost totally ignorant that our "public schools" are based on the principles developed by Prussians with a lust for absolute power and absolute control over others.

Americans have, like the Germans and the English (who also copied Prussian educational innovations), interwoven into our national psyche an unconscious adoration of power, whether we individually play the part of the wolves or the sheep in our economic drama about survival. We are unconsciously addicted to violence, to brutal competition, to cruelty, and to indifference.

Today, violence is the mindset of kids who play at killing day after day in video games. It is the mindset of the movie and television industry, which found that random, indiscriminate violence creates, for them, excessive profits. It is the mindset of educational bureaucrats who, for a little power over parents and children, sell their soul to the system.

There are other ironies that should be noted. The colonists fought a bitter war to free themselves from the bureaucratic control of England and English corporations operating in America. Ultimately, every state in this "free" nation voted for bureaucratic control of our children. And now, our federal government, through the Department of Education, directs what we call "voluntary" (there is nothing voluntary about it, for federal monies to state educational agencies can be cut off in an instant), national goals and standards (strict conformity always appealed to fascistic thinking), which every child must accept as the law of the land. We have centralized education, and put children not under the control of their parents or the tutor chosen by their parents, but under the control of a federalized, two-tiered bureaucracy, in which states now bend to the will of a national imperative to create dumbed-down, obedient conformists. Often, the parents' only recourse is to remove their children from government schools and seek the right of home education under the rules and regulations of their state and their nation.

We see that children in America are now owned by the state, as they were in Prussia. They do not only live under the laws of a government that protect their independence and freedom, but according to the multitude of exacting prescriptions of educational bureaucrats, politicians, and educational "experts" who care nothing about raising consciousness.

Is it not odd that Americans see a compulsory, national educational system still based rigidly on the Prussian model of absolute, fascistic control, a necessity for Democracy? What pretense! What hypocrisy! For over 150 years, Americans lived with total freedom of educational choices and maintained a level of literacy that cannot be approached today with all the mandated, up-to-date, scientific research and instruction by a host of fully certified teachers.

Students who attended the hundreds of common schools in early America were literate before they left the protection of home to enter the variety of schools of their day. They did not require 12 years to learn to read intelligently or to fail to do so. With no accredited teachers (just mom and pop, or a private, uncertified tutor), one or two years was more than enough to read and understand what most college freshmen cannot read today: the *Holy Bible*, Shakespeare, Milton, Plutarch.

In this country, most of us have been subjected to compulsory schooling. Forced schooling functions as an extended right of passage, 12–13 years in length. Forced schooling is one of the main ways we experience being conditioned. To some it may seem natural and right and healthy. From my perspective, it is unnatural and wrong and degrading.

It is part of the cure to wish to be cured.

~Seneca 4

In 1960, districts across the nation were persuaded to build schools without walls using the "open education" concept, employing new, open-education methods until the schools woke from their delusion and added, at a huge cost, walls to stop the incessant noise and chaos created by those just trying to be heard.

In 1983, with the publication of *A Nation at Risk*, the National Commission on Excellence in Education reported what many citizens already knew, that schools were failing, that 23,000,000 American adults were illiterate, that a great proportion of teenagers were functionally illiterate, and that the average freshman in college reads at the seventh-grade level. One governmental response to the bad news contained in *A Nation at Risk* was the Secretary's Commission on Achieving Necessary Skills (SCANS), under the Department of Labor, heralding "outcome-based education" (OBE) as the solution to meet the low-level, labor required by corporations. What was seen as a panacea for corporations (not for authentic education) became, however, the new educational model, the latest fascistic fad purported to save our national educational system from earlier fads.

California led the nation with its new "whole language" reading program that created, in California and the rest of the nation, a generation of children who couldn't read.

Always, always, behind the scenes of a new fad is the:

- "compelling" research by an "independent" college professor

- the hired-gun educational consultants, some key political players, and the businesses that profit by a whole new line of "products."

- retraining of teachers in the Prussian methods at public expense

- grants by the two arms of state and federal agencies along with a host of corporations awarding huge gifts to fund the "new" system.

OBE was the educational fad of the day. OBE is the new poison for an already failed system in which the content and spirit of education was mandated by federal and state agencies and supported fully by corporations. As many parents who have tried to make changes in the educational system know, decisions about education of children are rarely made by parents or by children or by teachers. Nor do ideas for reform come from independent schools. They are generated by administrators beholden to powerful people with agendas of their own.

The roots of Outcome Based Education (OBE) are often traced to the learning theories of B.F. Skinner, a Harvard professor who developed techniques (reward and punishment) to train pigeons to set off bombs. Skinner saw a way to condition human behavior, as well as, to control the masses more efficiently.

His ideas were taken up by Benjamin Bloom, who created "Mastery Learning" (as the system was discredited, Bloom substituted other names like "Performance Based Education" and "Restructuring"), a system focused on controlling student thinking and student behavior. Bloom investigated how stimulus-response conditioning can be used to indoctrinate children to make them believe anything one wants them to believe. A moral relativist himself, Bloom declared all opinions of truth and goodness are equally valid. In the hands of governmental agencies, "Mastery Learning" (or whatever is the newest name for it) claims to predictably control students' thoughts and actions.

William Spady, often called the father of "transitional OBE," created a variation of OBE that creates goals that sound wonderful, but can only be judged subjectively, goals such as "appreciates diversity" or "is a good family member." Spady was interested in programming student behavior and values on a global scale. He claimed he could predict the future needs of employers and train students to fit the slots in the workforce as business needs changed. He promised that with his system, all children will succeed; all receive an "A" each time they demonstrate mastery of a given skill. Subjects like English, history, and math should be abandoned in favor of a checklist of necessary job-related, specific skills that are wanted by corporations. In the end, all students will become compliant and obedient. Prussia reincarnated!

OBE is not education, although "E" stands for Education in its title; it is the programming, with computers and without, of particular skills. Conditioning can be done with little or no consciousness, little or no attention. Teachers are to become conditioners, programmers. Educators are to become trainers. Although OBE masquerades as education, it is not, in my view, education at all, only another sinister way to train all children for the lowest level jobs in corporations at public expense. Individual consciousness and independent thought are to be crushed in order to promote slavish subservience to authority. The new "uniform standards" preclude any authentic education that lifts and expands consciousness, empowers individuals, and connects students with the world treasures of literature, the arts and sciences, a historical perspective, and an ability to think independently. OBE is simply another attempt to tighten the noose of State control over the minds of children for the purposes of those now in power.

OBE, along with other practices in our "Prussian" education, is an affront to children, to teachers, to parents. It effectively nullifies all potential for individual freedom, parental authority, a free-market economy, an educated populace, and a spiritual life. OBE is just one more instrument of mind control and social engineering on the road to crushing the human Spirit and animalizing people.

Spady's goals were embraced by T.H. Bell, the head of the U.S. Department of Education. The intent was the complete restructuring of society, using OBE as the means. Schools were not to focus on education, but to develop human resources for businesses. In addition, the "restructuring" would change and align student beliefs and values so they could, without personal conflict, serve any future employer. Long live Prussia!

The National Association of Education, eager to develop new national goals, cooperated in creating President Clinton's "Goals 2000," renamed by President Bush as "America 2000." Others who took part in this cooperative effort were Benjamin Bloom, the president of the American Federation of Teachers, the Carnegie Foundation, the National Center on Education and the Economy, and others eager to promote nationalized education to all the state governors and state legislatures as the hope of the future. Long live Prussian America!

There is a telling contradiction between two promises of OBE advocates:

1. that the implementers of OBE guaranteed that every student will succeed in meeting the new standards

2. that OBE will raise educational standards.

In any system where success is guaranteed in advance, any real standards are meaningless.

The rigidity of today's educational system is such that only a refusal by parents to turn over their children to the control of school authorities will force a change. Already, the number of home-schooled children has ballooned, despite the initial refusal of school boards to allow parents to homeschool their children

Parents whose conscience could not abide what happened to their children when they entered school, were willing to take on the responsibility of defying the wishes of school authorities by educating their children themselves without any teacher training, a daunting task for many of today's families with two working parents.

We need a revolution in the educational system. The crisis in schools in America deepens and festers. Despite the fact that schools receive ever more financial support, ever more technology, the educational mentality does not change. Since the consciousness of educators about their responsibilities to their students remains the same, since educational managers still control the day-to-day operations and decisions of schools around our country, since parents exert little or no control over what is happening to their children, nothing evolves. The inadequate response to the school stalemate is always to increase state and federal control. Teachers are under the gun from embarrassed politicians and school administrators to make their children pass tests that measure the lower limits of learning. Without direction, they continue to apply the same strategies, only with greater force. There is simply no more juice in the lemon.

The evaluation of schools in the past usually included the amount of square footage in classrooms, in cafeterias, in recreational facilities, the availability of fresh air, the intensity of available light, the number of books in the library, the number and variety of school specialists, the number and kind of educational degrees held by the staff, and the measure to which the curriculum conforms to state standards.

Today's formula for evaluation calls for testing of outcomes. Each state lists from 35 to 150 outcomes. Each outcome requires that a test be constructed to determine whether a student has met the standard, whether the robot has been properly programmed. This jungle of testing has only begun to be addressed.

Toni and I have always judged The Well, in contrast, by the frequency of smiles and laughter, by the number of comments by one student in support of another, by the commitment and industry of our students, by the ability of students to think independently, by what the average child actually accomplishes in a day, by how much students express their individuality in writing, drawing, and math. We have judged ourselves by how much kids figure out on their own, by how much debate and discussions enlivened the classrooms, by how our students treated each other and how they treated their parents and teachers, by the students' attitude toward learning, by what percentage of students stay after school to participate in extra-curricular activities when they might just as well have gone home.

One hour of life, crowded to the full with glorious action, and filled with noble risks, is worth whole years of those mean observances of paltry decorum, in which men steal through existence, like sluggish waters through a marsh, without either honour or observation."

~Walter Scott

We assessed ourselves by what our students said about our teachers and our program at Meeting, by reports from parents about how much their kids loved or hated school, by how frequently our graduates visit us, and by how well they are doing in their next school. Why these measures? Because these factors reflect the consciousness that prevailed in our daily life together. Because consciousness is the key to authentic learning.

NOTES:

Chapter 5: Intelligence and Human Potential

Over the course of the thousands of years of human history, the masses of mankind have endured repeated humiliation at the hands of their masters and have braved innumerable, formidable obstacles in their development in order to attain a modicum of dignity and a sense of self-worth.

When this country threw off the yoke of Great Britain and proclaimed freedom from the restrictions which had been imposed on its people, America developed a new consciousness of limitless possibilities, of new avenues of individual expression, trusting that each man had the wisdom to make his own decisions, to profit by his or her own experience. A new, exciting awareness gripped this fledgling country.

Although most well educated Americans at that time had only a year or two of formal schooling, they read and thought for themselves as never before and never since. Teenagers became successful entrepreneurs and made their own decisions in the marketplace, adapting to whatever conditions prevailed. Individuals decided for themselves what was in their best interest. The thirst for educating oneself in political matters as well as in the search for principles of truth, abounded and defined the early years of our nation's history. Individual consciousness soared, and was the basis for a highly educated public such as had not been seen since the society of ancient Greece.

We must not forget, of course, the blight of slavery and the thralldom of women that demeaned both these societies. Neither classical Greece nor the early United States had fashioned a truly equitable society.

Consciousness flourishes in a society whenever informed individuals are free to follow their instincts, free to experiment. These times in history are rare and far between. Consciousness at the individual level, however, depends on many factors, including the need for a long, gentle, period in which to slowly develop awareness.

A few hours after a colt is born, it stands, walks, and leaps. Its physical capabilities are displayed and it learns to work in harmony with others within a day. The great intelligence and spiritual nature, its complex, instinctive knowledge and sensibilities, manifest shortly afterwards. Its nature and predispositions as an independent creature are certainly totally developed within a year.

In contrast, a human is born retarded and dependent. He requires a span of years from birth to puberty and beyond to become, in any sense, strong, independent, and truly functional in his surroundings. What the horse accomplishes in one year takes the human at least fourteen.

If man were made for slavery, for servitude, for following orders, or for being a worker in an industrial world, his development would have been rapid and sure. But his long period of dependence, in my view, allowed for the development of his singular outstanding capacity, consciousness. Otherwise his brain, like many other animals', would have fully developed in a relatively short time.

It is true that human consciousness can be almost entirely thwarted by abuse (such a delicate faculty it is), and man fashioned into an automaton, conscious only of his primitive needs and functions, so that, in effect, he labors, he eats, he drinks, he eliminates, he watches television, and he sleeps. His dull routine, rather than defining the essence of man's nature, speaks of the nature of his loss.

When man's Spirit is nourished and set free, he astounds; there is no limit to his creativity, his compassion, his accomplishments, his expressiveness. As a child he develops his talents, the love in his heart, the ability to choose wisely as he gains experience and fulfills his responsibilities to his mentors. As a young man he perfects his judgments, brings his talents to maturity, and decides on a path or creates a new path himself, following his own heart and his own intuition. He expresses his nature at every turn, with every movement.

To me, the most obvious educational truth, one I have witnessed a million times during my 40 years of teaching, is this: the average student will demonstrate high intelligence in many areas once his consciousness is expanded. I have seen scores of students with apparently no outstanding talents become exceptional students simply by changing their attitude, by questioning their belief in their own limitations, and by learning to treat themselves and others with respect. Their orientation changed and their sense of possibility expanded, awakening their need to express themselves in their lives to the best of their ability.

In a state of greater awareness, they were able to call on more resources. They appeared brighter, more responsive, more focused, and more motivated. This capacity for consciousness to ever expand refutes the notion that individuals have a set intelligence. It is clear to me that they do not.

And I have witnessed scores of other students who began with an obvious ability, but also developed into multi-talented, brilliant students, also by further expanding their consciousness. Since awareness has no limits, neither does the absolute potential of a human being.

NOTES:

NOTES:

NOTES:

Chapter 6: The Rise & Demise of the High School

by Toni Garland

In light of eternity we shall see that what we desire would have been fatal to us, and that what we would have avoided was essential to our well-being.

~Fenelon [1]

In 1970, we constructed the Upper Building at the Well in order to house our new high school. The crew consisted of Roger Garland, Jay's brother, as builder; Barbara, Roger's wife, and Jay and me. Our picture for the high school was one of cooperation, an inclusive atmosphere, great courses, individual respect, and of course academic achievement infused with incredible joy. We failed miserably in the area of Inclusion, causing us to close grades ten through twelve in June of 1972, after two wonderfully difficult and rewarding years.

We have all experienced a dashed dream, but if you are the one experiencing it, the time necessary to recover and stabilize after the demise seems to take forever. This makes life very difficult – and far less enjoyable – for those around you. In fact, at times almost unbearable. In 1973, the dream and the reality of The Well High School ended. It seemed a necessity in order to end the division among the staff and our high school students. The change afforded some relief, though, because we could devote our energy to our family and grades K–9 of The Well. Our energy had been depleted not only from the disappointment of failing to bring unity to the school, but particularly from our inability to shift – that is to say, achieve a new perspective. We rallied our spirits regularly, through working together, singing in large groups, laughing at our dour days, only to find ourselves slipping back into "zombie" mode.

Although the demise of the high school was swift and brutal, the choice to end the high school was, in retrospect, an overreaction, a mistake. One day at our usual high school Class Meeting, one very intuitive student demanded an explanation of why the school had a "shit list." They were asking why a particular group of high school students was seen by their teachers as inferior, unwanted, and disposable. This single student's brave challenge to what was, sent a shock wave throughout the school. It brought out into the open a schism in the high school faculty that Jay had hired.

Jay's mistake was to hire teachers who he knew were extremely intelligent and accomplished without investigating if these teachers were attuned to The Well School philosophy and its practice. As it turned out, several weren't. They refused to attend the high school's Class Meetings, or its meetings with parents and students. They thought that a significant group of students were academically ill prepared for their classes. Yes, according The Well's policy of Inclusion we admitted a number of students that needed remedial help. That policy when applied to grades 1-8 not only worked, but enriched our school as it diversified our student body.

We agreed to drop the high school the next year. A new "Van School" was formed around the teachers who were comfortable with hierarchy and a policy of exclusion. Many students in this smaller "Van School," ironically, were certified members of the "shit list," but were needed for the tuition their parents contributed.

Fortunately, the high school kids who lived with us for two years would graduate at year's end.

If we had to do it all over again, Jay would have fired these excellent but intolerant teachers immediately, expanded the teaching duties of a few teachers that favored Inclusion, and perhaps added a teacher or two.

In those days, we were much slower to recognize the gift hidden in events that seemed, or were, traumatic. In fact, if someone had suggested the term "gift" to me during a particularly stressful time back then, I'm not sure I would have heard them. If I did hear, I probably would have filed their remark under the heading of "Helpful Suggestions," i.e., those that seemed to be anything but helpful, such as someone suggesting that you *not* push when the process of childbirth has taken over your body. There are times when you totally resent good information. Was this ordeal a lesson? I might have been willing to chalk it up to a hard lesson. Well, maybe. Life experience? Of course! But, a gift? I don't think so.

If you let go a little
You will have a little happiness.
If you let go a lot
You will have a lot of happiness.
If you let go completely
You will be free.

~*The Art of Lovingkindness and Peace* by Jack Kornfield [2]

Jay and I experienced a particularly difficult period in our relationship during the time following the high school's end, each of us handling disappointment in our own way, mine being one of seeking friends and good times, and Jay's being of the nature of retreat and contemplation. I'm sure the reader can catch the rub right there. The closing of the high school seemed to parallel a divorce, with friends beginning to lean toward one camp or the other. Experience with and in our family life, however, continued to raise our own awareness. Together we arrived at new levels of understanding in dealing with disappointment. Comprehending and coping with the collapse of an enterprise was far less fun than creating it, although it was far more instructive. As our own personal understanding of responsibility in the dysfunction slowly came to light, new ideas could be shared through our classes, Class Meetings, and conversations that included friends, students, parents, and faculty. These often took place around the dining room table.

Hatred never ceases by hatred but by love alone is healed. This is an ancient and eternal law.

~Buddha [3]

The dining room table held an energy all its own. It was a large, trestle table consisting of two eight-foot barn boards with a thickness of two and one half inches that were seamlessly joined down the center to create an illusion of one gigantic slab of wood, replete with the rough outer edges of untrimmed lumber. The sturdiness of the table seemed to imply that anything could be spoken or done and the table could withstand it, while quietly supporting the people sitting around it. The well-finished surface exposed the swirls in the pine grain where large limbs had once grown. One looked like a graceful bird, nestled into the wood. Over the years, small holes were bored into the soft edges, as kids sat in the evening, working a pencil into its side while doing homework, or just talking. There is something irresistible about digging away at a dent or a hole. The surface, too, had its own imperfections: imprints of children's writing as they pressed their pencil too hard, leaving a copy of their name in the finish. (Occasionally, I would get out the belt sander and refinish the top, restoring the sheen and filling the holes with wood putty, only to have a new batch of petroglyphs appear.)

Over the dining room table hung a wrought-iron chandelier that held four candles. (We loved candlelight, so the dining room had many candleholders.) The chandelier also served as a note holder and a check repository. Since it was so centrally located, placing tuition checks or a note crammed into the chandelier was the quickest way to get it to the intended receiver. There were some who thought this risky, but it truly worked for us. Even those who feared the integrity of this device found themselves stuffing notes and checks between the wrought iron chandelier tongs, eventually succumbing to the efficiency.

Gathered around this table, with faculty and friends, on one particular day, I expressed my feelings of resentment and self-recrimination for having worked so hard participating in the high school, only to have it end. Usually, spirited "good mornings" were the order of the day, so when that wasn't the case, the lack of enthusiasm was swiftly noted.

"What's up?" Katy, our first-grade teacher, inquired as she poured herself a cup of coffee,

"I just feel so frustrated, I guess," I replied.

"About what?"

"Oh, I keep thinking about those kids who had to find another school. I'm just so angry that the whole thing is over. Some of those students gave their heart and soul to this school. It just feels like such a betrayal and, at the same time, I feel betrayed. Jay is so quiet, the place is like a funeral parlor housing an invisible corpse."

As we talked, Libby, our kindergarten teacher, entered the room, made a cup of tea, and sat down at the table. She got a quick update from Katy on our conversation. Then the topic switched. Libby had her own problem: a youngster in her class who pinched and bit. We talked about whether a child should be in kindergarten if he pinches and bites, and at the same time realized that something was clearly frustrating him. We were facing two problems: frustration, and how to deal with it in a civil manner. My mood lifted as I pictured this five-year-old surreptitiously squeezing the child in front of him in line. "God," I said, sometimes I feel like pinching the person in front of me!" Suddenly, the picture of me stepping up and pinching or biting my way out of frustration seemed hilarious. We all started thinking of times where a good pinch would have been the perfect expression of how we felt. "Yeah, how about that huge guy in the theater that has the choice of a thousand seats, and sits right in front of you! A good nip on the ear would have done it for me!" I confessed.

Libby got serious again and we discussed her biting student further. We realized we definitely needed a parent conference to make a plan as to how to help the youngster. Something was clearly wrong. This wasn't school behavior. Something needed to change. "I'll call and make an appointment if you want," I offered.

"No, I'll see his mom at pick-up and set a time and let you know," said Libby.

Knowing life is short, how can we quarrel?

~Buddha [3]

We headed to our classrooms. A child stepped to the front door to yell "School-Time," and the school day began. (One time, one of the kids wanted to call "School time" a coveted job by all and when he did, this little second grader added, "And get your asses in here." Thinking that was a little over the edge, we had a meeting later about swearing, picturing the idea that once we set the air into vibration, it continued forever. We came to the conclusion good language was a gift to the Universe. Later that day, another youngster was hit by a bat in her ankle as another child had excitedly thrown it, having gotten a hit herself. "SHIT!" cried the child with the aching ankle.

"Chris," I reminded. "Remember the meeting we just had?"

"Yeah, but Toni , this really hurts!" she moaned. I smiled to myself. You know, I could see her point.

My own frustration hadn't been resolved, but the atmosphere had changed. My resentment over the past had at least taken a back seat to the present. I walked down the hall, confident that this would be a great day. Why? Because I had mentioned to people I love what was on my mind, and because I could hear all the laughter and chatter of the kids as they entered the classroom eager to start the day.

As time passed, we saw other possible solutions for our resentment or self-recriminations. In those days, moving from the position of blame to the position of responsibility, and ultimately to a place of forgiveness, took a lot of discussion. The dining room table, I'm sure, heard a lot of blaming. It took us all quite a long time to realize that blaming created a victim mentality in ourselves that weakened our ability to act. The older I get, the quicker I go straight to forgiveness, knowing full well time is fleeting, and forgiveness is the inevitable outcome for any relief and peace to transpire. But, back then, we hadn't quite reached that conclusion. We thought we had the time.

Our desire to help children find their genius constantly prodded us to seek greater understanding. Jay and I shared a strong and binding interest to know about each other, others, and ourselves in relationships, intuitively feeling that the greater personal clarity we attained, the greater the possibility to reveal genius, creativity, and love in ourselves and in our students.

Jay's niece Tara, his brother Peter's oldest daughter, came to live with us the year following The Well High School closing. She was attending Conval, the local consolidated high school, and her disappointment at the closing of The Well High

School was somewhat offset by staying with our family.

In the 1960s and early 1970s, high school students frequently stayed with families other than their own. Of course, parents of high school students, our friends, and parents of Well students, Brooks and Carol, still had their share of kids. And the Eldredges' place was a home away from home for students. In the 1960s and 1970s, somehow there seemed to be a huge desire on the part of high school students to live apart from their parents' jurisdiction. For some, the "generation gap" was unbridgeable, for others, this provided an excuse to try something outside of home.

In later years, foreign exchange students took the place of "local exchange" students. Continued contact with the high school students through Tara, and the ex-Well students who went to ConVal, was great, but it didn't diminish the fact that our high school had closed.

Well has it been said that there is no grief like the grief which does not speak.

~Henry Wadsworth Longfellow [4]

Jay mourned the loss of the school, much like the death of a close friend; he became more and more pensive. Not realizing the forms that grief and loss take, I was sure it was I who was causing the sadness (a little egocentric on my part). I never considered the ending of the high school as a reason for his misery, although I am sure I was also a contributing factor. I responded to the loss by working harder and harder physically, to the exclusion of time for Jay. I brightened things up by applying fresh coats of paint to walls all over the house, busily making myself unavailable, and feeling a "tiny" bit martyred, sigh ... (it was a very big house, with a lot of walls). This excessive physical activity kept me going, but, spiritually and emotionally, it separated me from Jay.

As a couple, we became emotionally chillier and more distant with each other. I threw myself into tending to kids, teaching school, and cleaning. There were always endless things to do, so it wasn't hard to keep busy. Occasionally, the "air" would be "cleared" by a horrendous confrontation between us – usually instigated by me, I might add.

Fear contracts the heart. Its worries and anxieties stop the flow of love.

~Jack Kornfield [5]

Eckhart Tolle, author of *The Power of Now*, suggests it is the ego's need for drama that prevents us from discovering anything deeper in ourselves. We keep repeating the same drama, which keeps us from discovering a path to our inner life. In reading his book, I had to laugh at how accurately he described my pattern of "clearing the air." When I couldn't bear the tension any longer, I'd deliver a scathing report of the state of our marriage and Jay's shortcomings, seldom including any awareness of my own blemishes, while he silently retreated inwardly to God knows where – understandably. Mine were mostly the "sins" of commission, that is, saying outrageous things, hoping to get a reaction; his were the "sins" of omission, remaining silent, retreating, hoping the barrage would subside. It's difficult to have a conversation under those conditions, to say the least. I never saw the folly in this ridiculous sequence of events, nor the humor, until much later in life. Imagine two people with incredible love for each other, working together, living together, prizing communication enough to have it be a part of the school's core curriculum, and then creating a situation so "off the wall" or "less than loving" between themselves. Well, we did it.

Even though our dining room brimmed with faculty and friends, and our dinnertime hosted many interesting folks, camaraderie wasn't a cure for Jay's sense of loss, and certainly none of this filled the emotional void between us. Our rich friendships did provide a haven for me, and a place to find insight and humor. I discovered we weren't the only couple to have "bad days." The trick was to learn how to get through the bad days without leaving corpses everywhere; in other words, how to avoid saying ridiculously hurtful things that pierced the heart and were impossible to retract.

Yet, my frustration and anger grew. Although Jay and I did find time to get together, I had no clue as to how to fix our marital situation; the distance between us widened with each "air clearing." The void was powerful. We'd have a dinner date, and I'd immediately launch into the nitty gritty. "We can do this for free at home. Why go out?" Jay would observe, stimulating another barrage from me that, if not delivered right then, was tucked away for a more apropos moment. We grew more introspective around each other; the inability to comfort and receive comfort drove a wedge deeper into our relationship, translating into a wider distance between us.

I always loved Jay's ideas. I loved his energy. To be distant from him was torture for me, and yet I was a large contributing factor to the distance.

Marriage! Nothing else demands so much from a man!

~Ibsen [6]

Now, 30 years later, I can see that these psychic separations are a common experience in marriages or relationships. But, as a young woman, it felt to me as if this were a situation that only the two of us were capable of creating.

Even though the ending of the High School improved the honesty within the school by clarifying feelings and reality, the deadly notion of "if only" crept in, angering us and frustrating the healing process. "If only we'd done this, if only we'd done that" dominated our thought process, which led us nowhere new in our thinking. Unlike the divorce process, though, no lawyers had been engaged in the division to muddy the waters further. At least I didn't have to deal with the aspect of haggling over the remains of the school: who gets what and so on. There is a plus in everything.

> *Only when you start with what you have, do you find unlimited potentials within yourself. The action towards inner awakening can occur all of a sudden, or it can be gradual. But whenever it happens, it is contact with the living moment that knows no lack.*
>
> ~Tara Singh [7]

The true gift that arose out of our great distress may have been that the nasty pain finally drove us inward to discover the real resource, Spirit. As I mentioned earlier, considering disappointment as a gift was, at the time, a notion more to be ridiculed than to be considered seriously. Yet, during the fall of 1973, the notion of "love your enemy" slowly made sense to me. Having heard those words in Sunday school, they were all too familiar. Until now, that was where they had been left, Sunday School. I don't even know what brought the idea of loving your enemy into my brain, and I am even more in the dark why I chose to think about it. To pray for your enemy seemed totally hypocritical, since I was not in the frame of mind to wish well the people I saw as divisive or having habits I considered worse than my own. Resentment and the sense of having been taken advantage of were the devilish enemies I was trying to quiet.

However, I did find myself taking the time to pray for my enemy, just in case. Surprisingly, each time I renewed my gratitude for the whole nasty experience, the result was peaceful and heartwarming. At first, the peace I felt would last only a short time. Anger and frustration inevitably crept back in, mercilessly running the old "tapes of accusations" in my head, supplying the "if only" at the appropriate moment, surrounding me or us with a victim ambience. To find that there was recourse to these unhappy feelings through viewing the past in a new light and then letting it go brought instant relief, and eventually afforded us an opportunity for growth and change.

If it were not possible to free the heart from entanglement, hate, and fear, I would not teach you to do so.

~Buddha [3]

However, at the time, the negative feelings didn't transmute quite as readily as they seem to now when writing about it. Katy, Libby, and I often found ourselves in gales of laughter describing to each other the worst part of our lower selves that was provoked by certain conversations with our husbands. The heaviness of the feeling provoked in such encounters with our mates became lightened through humor and laughter, allowing us all to take a look at possibilities for change through more peaceful means. Rather than allowing things to build, and becoming accusatory, little by little, we encouraged each other to actually try to have discussions. Sounds easy and obvious, but often the obvious is the most overlooked.

I came across a story about two monks on a pilgrimage that depicted our own daily dramas. Both men dedicated themselves to God and vowed complete celibacy, promising never to touch a woman. On their pilgrimage together, they came to a stream whose crossing had become difficult due to torrential rains. A woman, distraught, stood on the bank, worrying about a means of getting to the other side. The older of the two monks told her to climb on his back; he would take her across safely, which he did. He set her gently on the opposite shore. The second monk made his crossing as well. The two monks continued walking together. Along towards evening, the younger monk, who had remained silent and mulling since the crossing, blurted out accusingly "I thought that we had made a strict vow never to touch a woman. You broke your vow back there by carrying that woman across the stream." "I made that vow and you made that vow," countered the first monk quietly. "I did carry the woman across the stream, but I left her on the opposite shore. You, my friend, are still carrying her." This was the continual challenge for us all. Accusation, mulling, and resentment wreak havoc in any relationship.

Judge thyself with the judgments of sincerity, and thou wilt judge others with the judgment of charity.

~J. Mason [8]

More space was available for the Upper School now that the high school no longer needed it. With the extra room available, Jay moved the fifth through eighth grades to the Upper Building. Until that time, our family and elementary school had shared the same space. Kambrah was in the sixth grade that year, so she and Jay "moved out." We no longer shared the same schedule in the same building.

One of the many things I missed was knowing the content of Upper School Class Meeting. It was always fascinating information, because the core of the meeting indicated how the school heart was beating. Now, the news update came at dinnertime because of the change in buildings. Kambrah and I no longer moved in and out of a mutual space.

Our all school Class Meeting tended to start slowly. Children, in groups of two or three, came into the room that was sometimes a stage, a classroom, or an art room. Students pushed the tables to the edge of the room, working together to flip other tables upside down, placed them on the standing tables in order to make more space on the carpeted floor. When tables or chairs were stacked, other students arranged and lit little candles that were placed in the center of the room as a reminder that light had the ability to push back the dark. Then students, faculty, and occasionally parents created a circle with the candles in the center. The room then became quiet. Sometimes, the quiet lasted for a fairly long period of time. Jay was a master in waiting. Occasionally, he would start a meeting with a short description of the Stoics or the Epicureans or something else that allowed the kids to compare their lives with a philosophy that was being described. A discussion followed.

Whatever you would have your children become, strive to exhibit in your own lives and conversation.

~Lydia H. Sigourney [9]

"Anyone have anything to talk about today?" Jay would inquire. Complete stillness settled on the room. No one moved. All the students waited, wondering who did have something to bring up and what would be the tenor of the subject? Was it praise? Was it confrontational? More quiet, until the silence was broken by a stir from a student over by the large, glass sliding doors. The rustle of his slippery, down vest revealed the speaker, and all eyes looked to see who it was.

"I know I have done this myself, but Amy, you are cheating in math class."

Amy's head whips up, her mouth opens but nothing comes out. Her face becomes flushed as she blurts, "I'm not cheating, Joel."

"I saw you write the answers from the answer book." Now Joel's voice is stronger and more confrontational. "I saw you go up to Jay's cubby and take out the answer book, look up the answer and write it down."

"When?"

"Yesterday, and today just before Meeting."

"I did not."

"Amy, I saw you do it, too," says her friend Pat. "You were in the hall, writing down the answers when I came out to get a pencil yesterday." Joel relaxes a little, since someone else has seen Amy cheating. He wonders why Jay doesn't watch more carefully for cheaters. In fact, he notices that Jay just seems to trust everybody. Jay leaves stuff all over the place that kids could abuse or get into and sometimes they do, but mostly they don't. Why doesn't he hide the answers?

"I was just getting a book myself," says Amy. "I can't believe you'd think I'd cheat." Pat is visibly feeling awkward for having spoken. Caroline, who is a grade above Amy, gets up and crosses the room to where Amy is sitting with her arms wrapped tightly around her knees, squeezing her body into a ball. Caroline snuggles in next to Amy and puts her arm around Amy.

"I cheated last year in history," Caroline says quietly. We all strain to listen. "It stinks when you're doing something dishonest."

"I didn't cheat," whispers Amy, as a large tear slowly makes its way down her cheek. Now, the whole room is aware that Amy did cheat. The room gets totally still again, and we all wait, hardly daring to breathe.

"I'm sorry, Jay," Amy whispers. "I did look at the answers, but I only did it twice." We all knew that if she were admitting to twice, we were catching on to a whole host of times, but no one says anything. Slowly, classmates come over to Amy, some telling of their own trials with cheating, others just reaching out to hug her. All of us cheaters realize the importance of stepping back on the path of truth.

"I feel awful," Amy sobs. "Does this mean I can't be in the play?"

"This has nothing to do with the play," says Jay. "But you say you feel awful. What do you need?"

"I guess I need help in math."

"Um," says Jay. "Let's have lunch and do a little math together." He gives her a big hug.

Silence again prevails, but all are relaxed.

"I love the poems you write, Arthur" says Augusta. I can't even imagine where your ideas come from. The description of our canoe trip was so beautiful. It especially amazed me, 'cause I thought you were just goofing off, smacking the water with the paddle, splashing us and laughing."

Arthur smiles, ducks his head and says, "Thanks." Usually, Augusta is telling him to "grow up," and this compliment comes as a nice surprise. He's a little embarrassed, but clearly pleased. Other kids in his class chime in their approval. "Yeah, cool poems." "Awesome" and so on. Often, when someone points out beauty or achievement, others see it more readily. Sometimes students "piggy back" on whatever someone is saying, either positive or negative. But, the students get pretty good at telling the genuine from the fake.

"Jay, I have a great book about Siddhartha. Could I read part of it for next Meeting?" asks Amara.

"Bring it in. Sounds good."

Reminders now come up about jobs. The perennial problem with the cleaning of the Upper Building toilets. Could the boys aim a little better? And so it goes.

"Jay, what about Student of the Week?"

Kids start naming classmates and telling why they think it might be that person.

"Julie, because she has done all her homework this week, has been a great friend, and helped the first graders get their skates on."

"No, but that's nice to hear about Julie."

"Is it Hank? He helped shovel the roof and has done three chapters in math?"

"No. But thanks for doing all that work Hank."

The time of guessing ends, sometimes students succeed in identifying the Student of the Week, sometimes they have to be told. Everyone cheers when they find out; the student makes a fancy name card at lunchtime and posts it with others on the wall. When five or six accumulate, Jay or Kate takes them out for lunch downtown together.

By now, the sun is pouring in the large, glass sliding doors; we are all just about melted, and mercifully it is lunchtime. "Let's have lunch and play a little ice hockey."

"Yeah!" comes a chorus of voices.

The Lower School teachers at The Well attended all classes with their students. If the class were singing, the students, their music teacher, and the class teachers all sang together. All gathered on the carpeted living room floor, teachers and older students held younger students on their laps and sang away. Jonathan, a parent and the guitar teacher, playing the guitar, serving up a variety of music for the students: rounds, folk songs, and traditional tunes. Everyone bellowed them out.

When a parent from Colombia enrolled a first grader, immediately we had a Spanish program: classroom teachers and students alike learned Spanish together. The classroom teacher had the opportunity to know what went on in class so that it could be enjoyed and reviewed later. The class teachers allowed the classroom teachers to become students within their own classroom, attending all recorder, soccer, ice hockey, art classes, as well as the academics. Although this was an usual practice at The Well, I understand that in most schools, classroom teachers feel their time is better spent elsewhere, while a special-subject teacher holds forth with their class. Our teachers enjoyed the information and the camaraderie afforded by attending class. Most of us looked forward to the special-subject classes as much as the students. I never realized that this total participation was unusual until the school had been established for thirty years and we hired a "real teacher" who felt that any time she wasn't "teaching" the class it was her time "off ". It presented a different flavor to her work. The beauty of a small school is that everyone is needed to make it work. Being there and learning along with your students gave the children the opportunity of seeing their teacher as a learner. It also gave me the opportunity to be in many of my children's classes, as was true with other teaching parents.

The grade teacher had the opportunity to see her students in a variety of settings, affording a new perspective of her students outside of merely academic abilities. It is wonderful to see the diverse ways in which your students shine, and once that light has been lit in one area, the chance of its glow spreading to other disciplines is very great. Also, the camaraderie of teachers supporting one another's efforts built a wonderful sense of trust and appreciation among the staff, not to mention the onsite laughter and joy that was available.

With the building change, Jay became the major influence in Kambrah's home and school life. No longer did I automatically know what her homework was. Now, I learned what her day involved only at the end of the day. At the time, I felt it such a privilege to know and participate in our children's day; but now, I realize the necessity and importance of parents keeping this kind of connection with their children. More and more, strangers and institutions are structuring our children's lives. The impersonal has become the norm for so many of our youth; sadly it can begin as early as three months when the child is enrolled into daycare.

Do not train boys to learning by force and harshness; but direct them to it by what amuses their minds, so that you may be the better able to discover with accuracy the peculiar bent of the genius of each.

~Plato [10]

Ak, our fourth grader, was still in the Lower Building, in my class. He and Kambrah maintained a close bond with each other, sharing in common family, cousins, friends, and school experiences. The change in buildings did not seem to interrupt their companionship. Music and math were his loves, although, as was true with the other students, he threw himself into building and crafts, and at eight, was just awakening to the pleasure of sports.

He became intrigued with the simple, homemade, manual-knitting machine that was an elongated spool-based tool. He built an extra long "knitting nanny," learned how to drop and add stitches, and made himself a vest, which he wore religiously. His ingenuity definitely impressed me. However, the loose stitch, the choice of orange and purple yarn, and the baggy shape appealed far more to boys than to me; just not my colors.

Students learning a craft together were able to get a host of varied results. Thus, they could use each other's ideas and expand on their own. Then, youngsters took off from the basic information, inventing and creating way beyond what the simple project presented, which in this case had been a knitted square for a class afghan made on an elongated knitting nanny. Instead of using a wooden thread spool, with four nails, and making a knitted rope, the kids made an eight-inch nanny with two pieces of wooden strapping separated at each end with a one-by-one-inch piece of wood. Each side of strapping had headless nails diagonally opposed one half inch, or so, apart on which they knitted afghan squares. Ak just developed the idea a bit further, which students did much of the time.

One Monday, a visiting basket maker taught students how to weave a simple, round, reed basket in class. The process caught Kip's imagination. By the end of the week, he had completed a large, finely woven bowl. He came into school the following Monday morning presenting his homemade, woven donkey and a woven whale, further inspiring the rest of us to new heights.

Great things transpired that year, even though we were working through our own personal heaviness. Music in the house, practicing and singing ringing through the dining room created a warm sense of hearth and home that was desperately needed. Often, the living room was wall-to-wall guitars, with five or six students playing together just for fun, or practicing diligently for the next coffee house. I loved hearing our own children play and sing together.

Yet, that year, family life was difficult for Danda, who was three years old. With Tara, Jay's niece, living with us, and Ak and Kambrah deeply involved in school, activities were often geared towards the older children, and it was hard for her to find her place. She couldn't, and really shouldn't have had to do so. Aspects of the terrible two's lasted well into the terrible fours. Frequently, what we did as a family group, she didn't want to do. "Contrary," would be the word I would use to describe her moods at that time. When riding in the car, four out of the five of us would lustily launch into a song, while a little voice in the back would peep out, "Please don't sing." And the stupid thing was, we stopped, expediently preventing a crying jag. The four of us were willing to buy peace at a high price. For the life of me now, I don't know why we didn't deal with her real needs at the time. Clearly, we were stuck.

We did begin to realize that things weren't going well for Danda, aware of the effect, but unaware of the cause. Somewhere deep within ourselves, I think, we as parents always know the real cause, but we just can't face it.

Each summer, the kids and I visited my family in New York. Jay generally opted to have this time to himself and, when you think of it, what husband wouldn't? "Would you like to spend a week with the kids and me at my mother's in an apartment in New York, or would you prefer to batch[elor] it and be on your own?" I don't really think there are two answers to that question.

At the beach club in New York, most of the members were total strangers to us. Yet, in this environment, Danda was off and running, enjoying the sand, sun, waves, and pool, and all the people. I noted, with some pride, how she didn't hang back, but took complete advantage of the entire club, even ordering lunch when she wanted something to eat. I noticed, more and more often, in large and unfamiliar settings, how easily Danda moved in and out. On the other hand, when we visited the households of our friends or her friends, in smaller or more intimate settings, the situation left her clinging to my leg or wanting to be held. Her comfort with anonymity in large groups became disquieting in contrast to displayed fear in smaller groups. I began to wonder what it was that she needed.

When our older two were Danda's age, we lived in a remote village in Alaska. There were far fewer constraints on Jay's and my time, far fewer diversions in the day to pull us in other directions away from the family. Life was much slower. Isolated in a small Eskimo village, where family life was our natural center, we didn't need to set aside time for each other. We all needed and enjoyed one another's company.

In today's busy world, a conscious effort has to be made to slow down the time. Eliminating TV does wonders; in fact, anything that beeps probably uses up time in an uncontrollable way. Even the clothes drier might qualify, since without one, you can bet we wouldn't wear so many changes of clothes!

Danda did get plenty of attention, but not always quality attention. Family life was abundant, but faster paced, and often involved extended family. She frequently got her "way" just to keep the peace. In reality, she got "nothing" in return. No wonder she was cranky at times. When I think of those two or three years after the high school closed, I think we, as a family, were all trying to survive – and Danda most of all. Since Jay and I were unaware of the reason for Danda's stress, it held great power, locking us into patterns of behavior that didn't work, even when we poured more energy into those patterns. One is apt to do that, you know – try to power through with an ineffectual tactic.

The reason angels can fly is that they take themselves lightly.

~Ken Carey [11]

In many ways, throughout the years, even though The Well required a lot of energy from us, it also sustained us when our own strength flagged. The closeness and love that developed among the faculty – Sue, Katy, Dorothy, Skipper, Carol, Peggy, Jonathan, Widdie, and many more – through conversation around our dining room table, school activities, working together, lots of singing together, and teaching allowed new perspectives for dealing with the everyday minutiae. A sense of emotional safety grew among us, lending a space to discover and talk about our lives without judgment. It probably wouldn't have happened as easily without such high stakes: the welfare of our children and our relationships with them. Somehow, we knew that the more honesty and clarity we gained, the greater the benefit to our families, and our classes.

Meet this transient world with neither grasping nor fear, trust the unfolding of life, and you will attain true serenity.

~Bhagavad Gita [12]

At these exchanges around the table, and also through parent, student, and teacher conferences, we discovered the importance of a mother letting the father and other authority figures connect with her child's life. Obvious, you say, but one would be surprised how often allowing others into your child's life doesn't happen. For parents, teachers, and others of that ilk to have authority over and a relationship with one's child is clearly important to the child's growth and development. To prevent that contact would seem a little irrational, somewhat stingy, or shortsighted, since we all know that "if you love someone, you set them free." Obvious or not, when there is a lack of trust or a grudge in a relationship, generally, both parties are unwilling to be generous with their things, much less with the people they love. One can readily see how confusing this is for the child, and how hurtfully children can be affected by this stinginess.

The mom holds the initial key to opening the world for the child. The day a child is born, traditionally, the mom, and only the mom, has the ability to nourish and comfort the child through her milk, nature's bond. Each new person the baby meets is subject to approval by the mom. If the stranger gets the nod of approval, he can become a member of the babe's circle, and the child's sphere is enlarged. Without her approval, the child's world remains static. For the healthy development of the child, the mom must allow the father to enter the inner circle, and together they share closeness with the child. But, unless the mother opens the door, the father remains locked out.

In every moment you plant a seed of one kind or another. That seed is going to grow. If it is a seed of selfishness, it is going to grow. If it is a seed of kindness, it is going to grow too. Which kind would you rather harvest in a few days.

~Ken Carey [11]

If the relationship between husband and wife is in harmony, the mother admits the dad to the inner sanctum at birth. Depending on the wishes of the mother, the dad may or may not be the first to enter the inner circle of mother and child. The mother may withhold her seal of approval for a multitude of reasons. The father may have been absent at the time of birth for any number of reasons, leaving the mother with a sense of abandonment. He may have been too wrapped up in work, unable or unwilling to take the time to be present. The parents may have forfeited their closeness during the pregnancy by forming new, intimate relationships with others (a thing that happens more often than one would like to think), causing the mom to shut out the father. Generally, resentment caused by holding on to the past keeps the door shut for the father if he wishes to enter. It's that young monk who is still carrying the woman: accusations and resentment get in the way.

Sometimes, the separation happens so subtly, the couple is unaware the division exists. In times of stress, our unconscious acts send loaded messages to one another, and this affects our children. In our case, many of these uncomfortable and unconscious messages were discovered through discussion among teachers, or among teachers and parents, bringing to light some of the effects they had on our kids.

When we, as moms, set ourselves up as the only effective comforters, we unintentionally isolate our children. We begin the process by being the only one to provide the breast milk, and we continue it by being the only one who "knows" exactly what the child likes. (The are some mom's providing the breast to their children in their thirties, mostly sons

129

I think. Scary observation.) We provide the "special" foods and cater to our picky eaters, remaining in sole charge of his nourishment for an unreasonable period of years, disallowing outsiders to offer sustenance. We thus magnify our own importance and keep our children dependent on us. Even when one discovers a pattern of control, a change is hard to make. In fact, seldom does one make the change willingly. The discomfort has to become so great, the dependence and the ill humor so tiring, that it makes one willing to give up the "special-all-powerful" relationship by trying something new and relinquishing the stranglehold.

> *The first ingredient in conversation is truth; the next good sense; the third, good humor; and the fourth, wit.*
>
> ~S.W. Temple [13]

By freely discussing what was not working in our own lives, parents and faculty helped each other see how to lead our individual lives more effectively. Our insights helped us to make conscious changes, freeing up our lives. The clarity that we gained – sometimes painful, often humorous—about our personal lives helped us with our children in the classroom, and it helped us with our families as well.

Frequently, when dealing with a problem in my classroom, I would find the same problem in our own household. The problem might be stinginess, sloppiness, insufficient effort, or any number of other issues. It was probably less threatening to see problems outside the family first, but once I noticed it in the classroom, often I found it was at home as well. What did these two situations have in common? Me. The realization that I was the problem always came last. Could I be stingy, sloppy, or lacking in effort? Moi? Yup!

I understood that the purpose of exclusive relationships was to keep control in order to prolong dependence, not really a very nice situation for either the parent or the child. But, although I understood this principle, I didn't apply it in my relationship with our child, Danda, until she was about seven. I turn red with embarrassment when I think of all the potato sticks Danda ate. Junk food never would have even been in the house the first 12 years of our marriage, but it worked as an effective – and timely – bribe for Danda, so I bought it. You could say that she introduced us to the stress of parenthood, although that is not entirely accurate. More truly, she became the channel for our stress. She illuminated how stressed we were as a couple.

I was so annoyed with Jay for not having the time for the children and me during the early years of Danda's life, my reluctance to let him into her life was strong. (Jay had been the ultimate father and mate during the babyhood of Kambrah and Ak, so his lack of time was strongly missed during the first years of Danda's life.) At the time, I did not actively plan to exclude Jay. I didn't wake up in the morning thinking, "Geez, let's keep Dad out of this or that." These things are seldom planned. We were building a high school building and interviewing students for the high school the first year of Danda's life. When he did have time for us, which in fact was probably more often than most dads during that era, I just plain wouldn't let him enter a relationship with our youngest child. How can you control your children's relationships, you ask? Hundreds of ways! Here are a few:

∞ When the baby cries, make sure to take the baby out of the father's arms and comfort it, making the father feel incompetent. (This works with anybody the mom does not want in the child's life: aunts, uncles, grandparents, neighbors, anyone.)

∞ Don't let him decide anything for the child; make him feel like he doesn't know enough when he offers suggestions or help; roll your eyes and sigh a lot; take over.

∞ Make everybody creep around the house when the child is sleeping, always aware that a time bomb will go off if a squeak is made.

∞ Keep the child more important than the spouse at all times.

∞ Stop all conversation when the child has any desire and give full attention to the wish.

∞ Interpret all interruptions on the part of the child as important needs.

∞ Be sure to get down on the floor to have a chat with the child at any moment, no matter what is going on.

∞ Any and all of these patterns are very bad news for family fun because the wrong order has been established based on exclusion.

Incidentally, Danda did have many people who were able to be close to her and comfort her. That was a blessing, but the key person, her father, was not one of them. The chain of command was out of correct sequence.

I clearly remember the day that I yelled "HELP" and things began to change. That is what it comes down to, you know. One has to be so uncomfortable in the existing situation that one is willing to make a change.

It was a March snow day, and school was called off – a rare thing in the life of The Well.

The snow was heavy and deep; the temperature hung just below freezing. By ten o'clock in the morning, the roads had been cleared. Some Well School moms and I decided to go to the local ski area and take advantage of the warm day and new snow. The Well had not had a ski program for a few years because the cost of fuel during the energy crisis caused the extra driving to be prohibitive. Consequently, many of the students at The Well did not know how to ski.

"Well," we all agreed, "What a great thing. We'll go skiing and all the kids can learn together." Off we went. Danda did not really want to go, but, well, honestly, was forced to do it. Not a great beginning. We got to the ski area, donned our equipment (not a simple process when resistance is paramount) and headed for the beginners' slope. We practiced on the bunny hill. With a lot of cajoling and encouraging, the rope tow was conquered. Danda had skied before, and she had been fearless, going 90 miles an hour down the hill, laughing and giggling on those few occasions, so it wasn't completely foreign to her. There had been a few years in between, however.

Later in the morning, pouting and whining began to set in more severely. There was no hope of her accepting help from anyone.

Here is a snapshot of us. Danda, sliding downhill, flopping in a heap at the bottom, and then turning her body into the consistency of a wet noodle. Danda turning her body into a limp, spaghetti-like heap, hair wild and snow in her mittens. Me, trying to help her up, beads of sweat forming on my entire body from overexertion and layers of clothing, seeing no humor in the situation, brow lined, molars grinding (it was a wonder I had any left) and being totally ineffective.

The marvelous mother-daughter experience framed in my mind in the early morning had vanished; now, it was a total nightmare for both of us.

Life has no blessing like a prudent friend.

~Euripides [14]

I remember Sue, a friend and mom who taught at The Well, skiing by, asking if I wanted help. "No," I said, not realizing I was in the same state as Danda, refusing assistance, and isolating myself.

Like mother, like daughter, but I surely didn't see it.

I remember leaving Crotched Mountain Ski Area. The two of us sat in the car, in total silence, teeth set, staring at the winding country road unblinkingly. Inside my head, my mind was whirling. "What's to be done!" The incredible love I had for this child was totally eclipsed by the stubborn separation of silence I felt as we rode home in the car. The silence created an ugly distance between us. What could be done? By the time we hit The Well driveway, tears poured out of my eyes mixing with nose goo and more sweat. Danda sat with chin to chest, sullen and sad. I felt awful. We made some picture, I am sure. Jay was in the dining room as we entered the house. Falling into his arms, all I could say was "I give up." Of course, Jay, naturally, was mystified, "Give up?" he said.

"It's Danda," I gasped. " Help!" I gave him a review of the morning, ending with the tear-sodden, thin-lipped ride home. The call for help let him "in." And help he did. The three of us sat down and talked. After some time, one of the results of the discussion was that, from then on, Danda was required to ask her dad for permission to do things: for rides to go places, for spending overnights with friends. Jay set up her chores, and became the parent in charge of everyday matters for her. What a difference, what a change! I could step back and see our daughter as an amazing human being. I felt total relief and gratitude. Sometimes, the solution is simple, such as providing more sleep, banning junk food, more fresh air and exercise, or a non-judgmental ear. Sometimes it takes a lot more; stop the judging, let people in; stop hoarding.

Whatever obstacles you face, never stop listening to the sound inside you. Do so and you are sure to lose the Way.

~Philip Toshio, *Sudo, Zen Guitar* [15]

A parent is in a very bad place when she is not enjoying her child, and the child is in an even more awkward situation, being smaller and less emotionally equipped to deal. It is the parent's job to create an atmosphere or environment that changes dislike to like. Naturally, we all love our kids, but like can be another story.

As in the home, so in the classroom: when the situation is not working, both parties – parent and child, or teacher and student – have to move to a new position. It is the responsibility of the parent or the teacher to be the first to move, but in fact, that is not always the case, but it is paramount to realize when someone has made a move. By the same token, a teacher must make the commitment to love her students. That's not always easy, but it is a pre-requisite for teaching children.

I jogged each morning before breakfast, often under the stars, Orion low and bright in the wintertime sky. As I ran down our country road, I'd picture each child from my class standing in a shower of opalescent light, the light filling up the youngster and washing over his or her body, clearing out any problems there might be held over from the previous day. I imagined the same cleansing for myself. This exercise of bathing away yesterday and starting fresh each day gave me an amazing feeling of love and connection for the students. There are endless ways to make this kind of connection, and gain a feeling of love:

- Appreciation circles, where each person tells the person on his left what he appreciates about the individual;
- Poems that uplift, said aloud together;
- Morning songs that generate positive feelings;
- Meditation – the list is endless.

You can give without love but you cannot love without giving

~Amy Carmichael [16]

Loving each student is a must. Otherwise, a teacher or parent has no business teaching, correcting, or criticizing. Remarks made without the ingredient of love and care are basically useless in terms of having positive results. It is never enough to teach or parent. There must be love.

In my case with Danda, control had to be relinquished. Letting go had been a long time coming. I had been so unaware. So often in my life, when I was frustrated by a method that did not work, instead of seeking a new method, I applied the old one with more force. (This takes the form of nagging.) Then, luckily – or at least I saw it as luck – something would come along and point out the absurdity of it all, knock me off my position, and reveal a new perspective. Each time, the new vantage point brought relief, and permitted a new opportunity for connection. Repeating one's self (i.e., nagging) clues one in to the fact that a position or mindset must be examined and changed. Nagging is directly related to "stuck."

Love turns into a vibration when it comes in contact with truth. Truth is matter. When truth and matter get together, we have the song of life.

~Ken Carey [11]

Exchanges with faculty and parents about such experiences helped us all to see when we were overbearing, incredibly controlling, or flawed in some way. Serious as many of these times were, our humor and laughter broke the spell of morbidity and delivered us from our "rightness." We could breathe and reconnect. After all, what was most important? Certainly the loving connection between people held precedence, and when I couldn't remember to love, someone else was there to remind me.

Other activities were of help in this way, too. During the high school years, Jay had established a Bible study group. Originally, he formed the group because most of the high school students were unacquainted with the teachings of the Bible. Lack of biblical background caused students to miss much of what was significant and symbolic in art and literature. During the late 1960's and early 1970's, much that might have been learned through religious studies at home or at church didn't transpire. Attendance plummeted in churches and Sunday schools, so the knowledge of *The Bible* among the student body was practically non-existent. *The Bible* study group, composed of parents and students, continued to meet for quite a few years.

The spiritual study became stronger, and the *The Bible* study groups lasted into the night, far longer than I did. (Sleep has always been a priority of mine.) Interest in Bible study grew, and a "Home Church" evolved. Each Sunday, five or six Well School families, sometimes more, met at someone's house. The homeowners prepared the service, but all joined in, reading, singing, or playing a musical instrument, most people bringing something to contribute to the Sunday meeting. The actual service was very beautiful, with rich readings not only from *The Bible*, but also from Gibran, Tagore, Tolstoy, and the like. Each family brought food for a potluck brunch following the service. The kids ate brunch in half the time that it took the adults to do so, and then played while the adults finished their meal and coffee.

I can't remember how long we held these Sunday meetings, but it went on for quite a while. The reading Jay and I did together, and the study groups we attended helped push us along towards a more conscious sense of Spirit. Although, for the most part, I still attributed most of the good that came our way to Lady Luck.

During that period, Jay decided to be baptized, one of several sacraments Jay's parents had ignored when he was a child. Actually, I don't think any of the sacraments held much weight in the Charles Garland household.

Jay seldom did anything by halves. By the time he had decided to be baptized, he was far better read in *The Bible*, and Bible-related material, than I ever had been – and I had two years of serious confirmation classes and endless years in Sunday School as a child.

A Well School parent was a pastor at a church in the neighboring town. He offered to perform the baptism. Of course, a large group attended the ceremony. The Home Church numbered about 30 or 35, plus there were others in the church congregation.

The spiritual experience certainly became evident in our daily lives, and consequently in the life of the school. Jay was given a huge, silver, Celtic cross that he wore around his neck. He looked like John the Baptist himself. Luckily, he did shave daily, so it was fairly easy to distinguish him from a prophet.

What we are is God's gift to us. What we become is our gift to God.

~Proverb

Talk of the Spirit, and spiritual ideas, began to permeate the school and our thoughts. This provided a new topic at the dining-room table. There were quite a few people for whom taking *The Bible* seriously was new territory. To witness the fervor and energy each book of *The Bible* inspired, was mind-boggling for me, especially since I didn't experience The Word as something new and revolutionary. The church and *The Bible* had been a large and positive part of my childhood and adolescence, so it was familiar to me. I had always loved the beautiful Lord's Prayer on which I have relied daily most of my life. (I love Anne Lamott's story of The Lord's Prayer referred to as "Howard's Prayer" by a child, "Our Father, who art in heaven, Howard be thy name").

Jay, however, had experienced no religious instruction as a child, growing up in a basically atheistic household. So, when he discovered Jesus and the parables, he examined them with his German-influenced thoroughness. This supplied endless material for dinner conversations.

Forgive Lord, my little jokes on thee! And I'll forgive Thy great big one on me."

~Robert Frost, *Cluster of Faith* ₁₇

The Well has never been a "religious" school. Spirit, however, has always been welcomed. As the years unfolded, Spirit became a stronger, conscious presence. In the early stages of The Well, searching for truth and Spirit provided a wonderful connection with each other. It became clear to Jay and me that there were many paths to Spirit.

In those years, C.S. Lewis was read on every level throughout the school. Beginning with the Narnia series, read in the early grades; *Till We Have Faces*, read in the upper grades; and *Mere Christianity,* read by teachers and parents. C.S. Lewis had a strong, beneficent effect on us all.

The children in my third-and fourth-grade class collectively created a huge tile mosaic of

The Peaceable Kingdom, complete with a lion, bunny, bird, huge sun, and goodness knows what else. Often they sang Donovan's "Brother Sun, Sister Moon," among other songs, while working together cutting and gluing the ceramic tiles. The scene of the kids singing and working together in harmony in the hallway outside of our classroom was just a little short of idyllic. Did we still have teasing? You bet! And discussions about hoarding the special-colored tiles. We all remained very human; we still needed all the help we could get.

Once someone called The Well for information about the school. The mom was very upset by the playground behavior of the children in her youngster's current school. She wanted to know if we had teasing at our school. "Did you think you dialed heaven?" I asked. Yes, we had teasing – at times. Teasing managed to be a recurring topic then, in Class Meeting, just as it is today.

After Barley's death, in the winter of 1974, the Home Church withered from lack of necessary energy to organize each Sunday gathering. My need for quiet and space in an otherwise community-oriented week led me to seek the peacefulness of an official Sunday church service. Part of the appeal was that someone else was responsible for the program. Another draw for me was that no one else in our family was interested in going. I thought this hour a week – by myself in a congregation, ideal, a real respite. It was a time of responsibility to Spirit only. Of course, the whole thing snowballed, and before I knew it our whole family was attending the service. To compound our involvement, Liz, the eldest daughter of our friends Brooks and Carol, married the minister of a church, catapulting – or so it seemed – Jay and Brooks Sr. into the positions of deacons, or were they elders? There they were, Brooks and Jay, passing the collection plates each Sunday, the rest of us looped into the whole church community. So much for my isolated, non-peopled Sunday hour!

With the union of Liz and the minister, we were all involved in the whole church community. Just exactly what I didn't need: more community. And believe me, church affords a lot of community. My hour of quiet retreat each Sunday evolved into obligation, something I have never been good at fulfilling gracefully.

When Liz, although very young, decided to marry the minister, it seemed like a good idea to Brooks and Carol, and Jay and me; we all had married at very young ages, and had been glad of our early commitments. But marriage isn't for everyone, we were to discover. That turned out to be true for Liz, but not until we had all put in a lot of church time. You would have thought that the current statistics about divorce would have been a serious clue for us.

We went back to studying *The Bible* and other holy books in small evening groups. Our brief foray into the realm of organized religion ended with Liz's separation. Brooks heaved a huge sigh of relief, in a way, content to have his Sunday mornings back for woodcutting, gardening, or other outdoor chores, which in the past had been his Sunday cathedral. Truth be told, we all were glad to reclaim our Sunday mornings.

Civilization: A limitless multiplication of unnecessary necessities.

~Mark Twain [18]

One Sunday morning a few years later, our son Ak and I were driving together down Concord Street, a road that sports quite a few churches in our small town of Peterborough. Cars lined both sides of the street, and people were making their way into the place of worship of their choice. "Why don't we go to church anymore?' Ak inquired, somewhat wistfully.

"Things change," I mused aloud, and we slowly drove on, each quietly and fondly recalling our own earlier Sunday memories. That very afternoon found us in church, attending a nephew's First Communion. Sitting next to me in the pew, Ak leaned over, sweat dripping down his sideburns, a result of the heat of bodies touching, pressing together in the cramped quarters and dress clothes. He whispered in my ear, "Now I remember why we don't go to church." We both smiled with mutual understanding.

The fall before the absolute end of our "Church era," Jay became very sick. He contracted a horrendous case of the flu. He had slowed down considerably the summer before, still putting in long days, but pacing himself to do so. Prior to the onslaught of the flu, his face and hands had become very puffy and his skin had a yellowish cast. He was always cold. He wore a heavy wool Norwegian sweater throughout the summer. His physical responses were slowed and deliberate. He would stop the car in the middle of traffic, take his time to look around to get his bearings, cars whizzing by or impatiently backed up, and then he would slowly decide which way to go. My toes curling, car horns beeping, afraid to look either right or left for fear of what might be coming, I rigidly prepared for the crash staring straight ahead. I was sure we'd be rear-ended or slammed into by traffic from either direction.

Rotaries were a nightmare! Cars flew by, spinning off the rotary, accelerating with centrifugal speed as we sat in the middle of traffic and studied the area to get our bearings once again. Jay would be calm as a cucumber, or at times vexed at peoples' "rudeness" as our car sat there, a stationary island amidst a sea of madly rushing cars. Hard to believe, but we never even experienced a fender-bender. Divine intervention, I'm sure now. Back then, Lady Luck got the recognition.

In conversations, I felt I could smoke a whole cigarette between my question and Jay's response, and sometimes I did. Sometimes I wonder at the gods' sense of humor, as surely as they must question mine at times. But, to allow Jay to become more calm, more deliberate, more contemplative, when he was the one with ultimate patience in the first place, seemed like a cruel twist for a mate like me, who wanted everything done yesterday, including quick responses, and a "moving it right along" modus operandi.

When Jay's flu intensified, I became adamant that he see a doctor. I feared it might be another attack of pneumonia, a disease he had almost died of in Alaska. A friend and minister from the town church was wonderful, teaching some of Jay's classes for him, and strongly encouraging him to see a physician. The whole school rallied, helping out with classes, older students taught younger students, parents came in and took up the slack wherever they were needed.

Seeking medical advice would have been an automatic response in most families, but not the Garlands. Doctors were the very last resort. Orange juice and vitamin C was the basic cure for everything in the Garland household. (Clearly, a legacy of Barley's influence.) Finally, we did get Jay to a doctor, who found his lungs to be totally clear of any fluids. That crossed out the possibility of pneumonia. However, there were some other signs that weren't good: internal bleeding, no ability to make blood; extremely slow reflexes, and very poor circulation; hair and hearing loss, and lack of coordination, to name a few. (No wonder the beeping horns didn't bother him.) Tests and more tests were taken. Of course, it sounded like cancer to me, but our doctor warned me not to jump to any conclusions until all the tests were in. "Right," I thought. "Just how is that done?" I did jump to conclusions, and the two weeks it took to get the test results were agony for all of us. I couldn't imagine my life without Jay; I found myself pushing that very picture out of my mind. The only good news was that Jay's flu had subsided. Vitamin C and orange juice had done the job.

I found it hard to look at Jay without crying. We were caught in the anxiety of the unknown, and to me, with all these horrendous symptoms, death seemed imminent. Finally, just when we could stand it no longer, the results of the tests arrived. The diagnosis was a non-functioning thyroid that, it turned out, could be easily remedied.

What a tremendous relief! We laughed, we cried, we hugged, and I danced around wildly. He was told to take thyroid medication, and in about a month he would begin to feel better. Of course, immediately, we all felt better knowing Jay's illness could be managed medically. Apparently, this condition had been worsening for the last three years, but so slowly the daily decline was imperceptible. I had attributed the slowed reactions to a conscious choice on his part. I thought it had more to do with a changing lifestyle: intentionally becoming quieter and more pensive, more contemplative.

That proved to be totally incorrect. Within two weeks of Jay's starting to take the thyroid medication, he had lost his yellow hue and his puffiness. He started to lose weight and regained his energy. By the third week, he was organizing after-supper ice hockey games. At the end of the month, the rest of us were wishing we had a thyroid problem and could have some of that medicine. People would meet Jay downtown and, not exactly recognizing him, ask him if he had a brother named Jay. The change, so dramatic and wonderful, filled us with total gratitude. We had been given a new life, and our family welcomed it with open arms. We laughed again. Things had been so serious for so long. Joy, a most necessary ingredient for life, can slip away so slowly one doesn't notice, but when it returns, and laughter once again becomes a part of the conversation, gratitude flows, and a sense of well-being presides.

There is no genius in life like the genius of energy and activity.

~D.G. Mitchel [19]

With Jay's energy refurbished, and spring on the way, all thoughts turned to plants with a force never before experienced at The Well. The Upper Building stage area became occupied with wall-to-wall peat pots, starters for little seedlings. Jay and the students hung planters all over the building. One or more of the jobs was to water the seedlings, another to water all the hanging and potted plants. You can imagine the fun the kids had with the water sprayers. Job time became unapproved interludes of water fights with misters. Plants, flowers, vegetables, and herbs occupied every square inch of the Upper Building that tables and chairs did not. Kids were taking cuttings of cuttings, creating more and more plants. Kambrah's bedroom looked like the tropical rain forest. Ak had sweet peas growing up the posts on his bed. A huge, flowering, lavender lantana plant hung from the ceiling over his bed. He built a wooden planter into one corner of his bedroom that housed a cacti garden.

During Project Month, Ruth Pittman, the art teacher, and her students made a beautiful, circular, herb garden replete with a stone path and a birdbath in the center. Plants were everywhere that year, and for years to come.

NOTES:

NOTES:

CHAPTER 7: DEATH OF OUR ROCK: BARLEY

BY TONI GARLAND

In 1974, Jay's father, Barley, died. He had been failing, finding it more and more difficult physically to get around and to stay warm. His discomfort and despondency left us all at a loss as to how to be of help to him. When he died, we all felt great relief for him to be free of his physical suffering, although the thought of him not being around left us more than a little off center.

> *Were a star quenched on high, For ages would its light still Traveling downward sky, Shine on our mortal sight. So when a great man dies For years beyond our ken, The light he leaves behind him lies Upon the paths of men.*
>
> ~H.W. Longfellow, *"Charles Sumner"* [1]

Actually, Barley's death left us reeling, which surprised us all, since in the more recent years he had held such an emotionally detached presence. Through his death, I discovered how a patriarch holds a family pattern with an intangible force, much the way the sun affects the planets. The difference is, one learns in the elementary grades about the physical forces of the universe and their effect on objects; no one mentions the family forces of order and energy, in or out of school, or, for the most part, anywhere else. This is information one must discover on one's own.

Bickering did take place over the inheritance of Barley's estate, complicated by a mixture of ten legitimate and illegitimate children. That in itself is a humorous thought to ponder. How can anybody be illegitimate if the parents know it is their child? But the most unsettling and disturbing effect of Barley's death to the whole family was the loss of the "sun" as our governing body. Our gravitational fields were disrupted, leaving us wobbling in orbit. We all knew and respected Barley's values: quiet, gentle, kind, and detached in life, Barley held the space for those values that subtly gave tremendous strength to the constellation of the family.

Nobody fell apart; everyone still functioned very well, yet I felt our whole routine and life shaken to the core, and it surprised me greatly. When the order is disturbed, chaos doesn't necessarily follow, but much more energy is required to maintain forward movement until a new order is realized.

Jay's father's ideas permeated our family and strongly influenced the way that we all lived. Deeply affected by the works of Leo Tolstoy, Barley loved simplicity, mistrusted government (or any authority, for that matter), and revered and honored the common man. His abilities, which made him a master philosopher and a master mechanic, enabled him to live very independently, and with an emotional detachment stronger than most men.

Don't part with your illusions. When they are gone, you may still exist, but you have ceased to live.

~Mark Twain, *Following the Equator* [2]

Barley was convinced that man created his own reality, a notion new to me in the 1950s and early 1960's. This idea was the basis of his winter writings. Earlier philosophers wrote about this, but the idea of creating and being responsible for your own reality wasn't a very common belief in the 1950's. Barley, however, had held to it strongly, writing daily in the winters, recording his thoughts, then putting his writing aside in the summers in favor of outdoor work.

A single candle can light a thousand more without diminishing itself.

~Hillel the Elder [3]

Barley's death was for me was an example of how integral a force each human being is in a group; it made a lasting impact on me. I began to notice group dynamics everywhere: at school, at home, and in the community. The equal importance of each member in a group, regardless of his or her place in the social or academic pecking order, became obvious. The apparent weakest held the same value as the most powerful. The power of the circle gained further significance; the notion that each member sitting on the circumference was able to witness a different perspective, and offer a slightly different view of a situation, came to light. Each observer and observation held as much value and weight as the one to the right or to the left of that position; each was of value.

An era can be said to end when its basic illusions are exhausted.

~Arthur Miller [4]

NOTES:

CHAPTER 8: HOME AND SCHOOL LIFE

BY TONI GARLAND

In the spring of 1975, Sue Chollet arrived at The Well with her clipboard. Sue was poised, energetic, athletic, quick to flash a brilliant smile, intelligent, and a practical joke lover. However, all of these charming characteristics were well disguised as she meticulously investigated schools for her first grader, taking notes and asking questions. Her serious demeanor was emphasized by pen in hand and legal-sized yellow-lined paper, attached impressively to a legal-sized, brown clipboard. Several ruffled pages revealed copious notes. I don't believe we have had a parent before or since so prepared to review every feature of the school. Goodness knows what all her questions could have been, but it was clear that she had carefully recorded the answers in detail for later rumination.

Apparently, there had been bullying at the pre-school her son had attended, and Sue was determined to have him placed well and safely. She required a good program and a safe place, both admirable requisites. After at least three school visits and many phone conversations, I said to Katy, our first-grade teacher, "If that woman calls one more time, tell her we are full." Sue was beginning to look like a lot of work to me. Fortunately, she didn't call again, and she did enroll her son Chris in first grade. Consequently, the aforementioned stellar characteristics were revealed to us as Chris's membership at The Well lengthened, but not before one memorable phone call from Sue, during which she pointedly reminded me of the bullying experienced at Chris's previous school. She feared the bullying might start up at The Well. I said I would keep an eye out, and I asked if her little boy were blond. (It was at the start of the year, and we were still becoming acquainted with the new students.) While engaged in conversation with Sue on the phone, I looked out the window watching Katy, our first grade teacher, hurry toward a tree with a group of children in it. A little blond boy was standing on the ground under the tree with an enormous stick, whacking at the children in the branches above, hoping, I think, to dislodge the climbers, or at least frighten them. I described the child's clothes and the activity. Yup! That was Chris, Sue's son. Wonder of wonders. Could he be bullying? Had I not eaten so much crow in my life, it wouldn't have been so humorous to me.

We both laughed. At once, she revealed one of her best characteristics: she could laugh at herself. Sue volunteered time to bake with the first and second graders that year, which was the start of her long and wonderful career at The Well, and the beginning of a dear friendship.

That same year, Jay and I had gone to a weekend that the Catholic Church sponsored called Marriage Encounter. I can't remember who told us about it, but it was to be another eye opener. The Catholic Church provided a weekend designed to enrich working marriages. It was not billed as a remedy for poor relationships, which was appealing; there seemed to be so few things that promoted and aided a "healthy" marriage. At that time, most services or counseling were for relationships that were in troubled times or on the rocks. One of the biggest gifts of the weekend was that we spent uninterrupted time together – something few couples have – discussing things that just pertained to us as a couple. The facilitators put forth questions, and we, in turn, discussed them through letter writing to each other. It was a simple idea that could easily have been done at home, but who would? We heard each other in a way that we hadn't in years. Through this process, we realized that our marriage needed a lot of work. Our family order was out of whack.

The Chinese are perhaps the clearest about the role of first to last, oldest to youngest, in the family. In the hierarchy of the family, each person has his birth order with specific obligations and privileges. When each person knows his place and accepts it, relationships and activities can operate smoothly. When individuals attempt to usurp another's natural role, tensions and anxieties arise, creating havoc and chaos.

What families have in common the world around is that they are the place where people learn who they are and how to be that way.

~Alva Myrdal, Viola Klein, *Women's Two Roles (1956)* [1]

For example, when the younger brother wants to be treated like the older brother, he usually wants the older brother's privileges, but probably not his responsibilities. He pushes to take his brother's place, being dissatisfied with his own. Everyone intuitively understands the natural order. Each position in the family has its privileges, importance, and its job simply defined because of its place. No one can take the place of the first-born. Often, in an attempt to be "fair," parents will elevate the next child to be in the first child's place, leaving number-two spot empty, and overloading the firstborn position. The first-born attempts to defend his or her place. The anxiety that is created by allowing this to happen is unnecessary. The first child has duties: as an example to break ground for the rest of the children, and to be a liaison with the adult world. The role of second child is to support the oldest and, in return, he can walk the path more easily created by the elder.

The idea of family order was extremely interesting and became very useful at family conferences, as we understood more of the ramifications of family placement. No position was better than another. Each has its own perspective and importance.

At Marriage Encounter, we discovered that although we were parents, often we were not at the heads of our family. Somehow, our youngest, Danda, had slipped into that position. She was allowed to interrupt and change the direction of the conversation at any given moment. We realized she decided things that shouldn't have been in her power to decide. This wielding of borrowed power exhausted her, frustrated her with tantrum-provoked decisions, causing tears and unhappiness.

When parents are bickering or emotionally separated, unwittingly, children are apt to slide into the space between the parents, allowing things to slip further out of control. Sometimes, a child is "invited" into the place normally filled by a spouse who is beside him or herself with loneliness.

Jay and I, unaware of the magnitude of our separation going into the Marriage Encounter weekend, surprised and shocked ourselves as we experienced this discovery.

Earlier that year, Kambrah and Ak had walked to visit the Whitehouse's, who at that time lived six or seven miles away. Tension between Jay and me had become so unbearable for the kids they'd sought refuge with Brooks and Carol. You might think that would have awakened us to their concerns. Luckily for us and for the children, there were other people for them to turn to. Indeed, not just people, but folks who loved them and loved us, too. It does take of village to raise a child. I must say, however, that at the time, I thought that our kids were overreacting.

Making comparisons can be an insane way of understanding a situation. When I compared our household to the one of my childhood, our current situation seemed far more peaceful. From my perspective, our New Hampshire home was heaven. What could be so upsetting to them? Their father wasn't abusive, or an alcoholic, or a hilarious partier – that was my dad, until he got home and transformed into an angry, guilt-ridden tyrant, or a flamboyant businessman hosting in-town, two-martini lunches and rolling home in the early morning hours laden with night club memorabilia: Stork Club ashtrays, swizzle sticks, and packets of Sensen breath fresheners to keep people from suspecting he'd "had a drink." The lobster-red face and the list as he walked just might have been suspect in the wee hours of the morning. Our children weren't awakened with inebriated shouting and slamming of pots and pans against the stove, grease sizzling and spattering as the flank steak hit the hot wrought iron frying pan at 3:00 a.m., my dad singing the latest popular tune, recognizable only by the words, since the melody was basically missing in his rendition of any song. (As a kid, I always wondered what he could be hearing that the rest of us didn't when he went to a musical or listened to the top-20 popular hits on the radio.) Tension? To me, that represented tension.

Forgiveness means giving up all hope of a better past.

~Jack Kornfield [2]

Here is the kicker: our kids weren't making comparisons. They couldn't even if they had wanted to do so. They hadn't been there in the household of my youth to experience what it was like on those occasions. But they were seeing clearly and feeling strongly as I wasn't, that the tension between Jay and me was unbearable. It was making life hell for them. It wasn't until later that I realized how deadly such "holier than thou" comparisons are. Blinding! You can't be better parents than your parents, and there is no point in going there. You can become aware of the present, however. Growing up is letting go of the judgment of what one has experienced in order to see what is happening now. Growing up is a continual challenge. Choosing love over and over again leads to the tranquility we all desire.

When we decided to go to the Marriage Encounter workshop, Jay and I thought we were going just to enrich a good partnership. After all, we had been married for 13 years, longer than the national average – another useless and meaningless comparison, by the way.

Through questions set up by the facilitator, we were able to see qualities about each other that had been eclipsed by the day-to-day process of life. We began to realize we hadn't been very good to each other for quite some time. Only when Jay and I were able to realize the distance that existed between us were we able to make the decision to close it. It was that simple; we just chose to do so.

Joy and love followed, almost like a new marriage. That sounds so sappy, but it is actually the simple truth. At that time, I was beginning to suspect that we choose everything – the powerful notion of choice that was just coming to light in my consciousness.

Strange as it may seem, along the path of our life together, Jay and I have seemed to stumble into classes or books or weekend retreats or people that have led us to set a better, more fulfilling course together. Robert A. Johnson in his book, *Balancing*

Heaven and Earth, refers to these path directions as "Golden Threads." The Marriage Encounter weekend became another solid stepping-stone, a Golden Thread for us.

> *The peace and stability of a nation depend upon the proper relationships established in the home.*
>
> ~Jade Snow Wong, *Fifth Chinese Daughter, 1950* [3]

Through writing a series of intimate letters, we became safe and secure again, having reopened the lines of communication based on our love for each other. Opening our eyes to joy and love is the key. We realized we needed to re-establish our authority as parents from a place of love, not a place of control or expediency. We put our heads together, took charge, allowing discussion to take place once again in the family. We took a long and careful look at our family, gratefully acknowledging the wonders of our children and seeing how we, as parents, needed to change the order in our family to allow the greatness in each person to thrive. Once we as parents set our intentions and pictured greatness in our household, magically energies changed and greatness was once again alive and well in our home.

We had taken such pride in our children, our wonderful lives, and each other, that it was hard to even notice, never mind admit, that everything wasn't wonderful and under control. Actually, it was under control, and that was the problem. Our weekend provided us with a rude awakening when forced to communicate through intimate and gentle letter writing.

We laughed on our way home as we realized what arrogant and blind fools we had been. And, we committed ourselves to a change. Painful as the realization had been, the fact was, nothing could have improved until we saw the problem. And, in order to see the problem, we had to take a closer look and see more clearly what was really going on in our lives.

> *What has made this nation great? Not its heroes, but its households.*
>
> ~Sarah Hale, *Traits of American Life (1835)* [4]

The information we gleaned from this experience became very useful in parent conferences. Because of our first-hand acquaintance with the principle of family order or, I should say, our family disorder, we saw readily in conferences with parents and children, when the order in a family was out of sync. We had felt tremendous relief as a couple when we finally came to reorganizing our own priorities and family roles. It was our hope that the information would help other families as well.

There are so many avenues for families to slip out of order: the first, and most obvious, as was the case in our family, is when parents become emotionally separated, and a child (or children) fills the void.

Families with one child can experience order-displacement, too, although it can be more difficult to recognize. If, in a family of three, there are two parents and one child, sometimes the child is elevated to the role of parent. There are more than a few adults that want to be children once again, confusing the order. Again, when disorder takes place, tension and anxiety abound. It is harder to detect in the early stages of a trio, because often, single children aren't asked to share, or take responsibility, or give up space the way they naturally would in a larger family. There isn't the need. When the mother or the father avoids the personal responsibility and slips into the role of the child, that transformation mystifies everyone involved, causing all to be off balance. We've all attended restaurants not of our choice, but because it was the choice of a potential tantrum maker or pouter if he or she didn't get his of her way. Many of us have watched more than one sports event simultaneously on TV as the clicker holder, usually the dad, surfs the channels while the other viewers try to keep up with color of the uniforms as a clue to what they are watching. Are decisions being arrived at through consensus or fear of potential bad behavior? Incorrect family order improperly places the power in inexperienced hands, creating jealousies and chaos. Correct family order can dispel a great deal of this tension.

An example, written about by one of my students in his journal – all my students kept a daily journal – concerning his older sister who also attended The Well. The description awakened me to how family disorder can be discovered not by the parent or interested adult, but by the child himself:

> *Grappling for some scissors I believe belonged to me, while Joy struggles for them on the other side, I realize the foolishness of our battle. It is just another foolish squabble between my sister and me and being young, neither one of us will give up until we win. Joy, my older sister, demands that I relinquish them. The sounds of our argument reach Mom in the other room and soon she is reprimanding my sister. Being only six, I shrug off the incident and move on to find something to eat. Within my heart, I am still confused as to why Joy took all the blame for our fight. I wonder if I would have taken the blame if I were the older one, or if Joy still would have been forced to take responsibility.*

> *Although this scar originated when I was fairly young, I didn't truly understand it*

until several years later. It took me some time to figure out, piece by piece, this problem of being favored. With each part came more and more pain, but at the same time, more understanding. I'm sure even now I can't grasp the entire meaning of it all, but I know more now than when I was six. This problem of being "favored" is something I always felt uncomfortable about.

It was an uneasy feeling to think and wonder why I got in trouble so little, while I did cause much. I really didn't understand why I seemed to be favored through any disputes. It even bothered me to the point that I'd confess to my parents that I was the one creating the troubles or arguments. Often the older sibling is expected to take more responsibility; still I couldn't figure out why I seemed to be favored over Joy.

Being treated differently was a scar that developed more over the years, for I would often ignore it. Because this was rarely discussed, sometimes I forgot about the problem – until it arose again. Although I knew Joy would get hurt taking so much of the blame, she never spoke much about it. However, I would occasionally hear comments pop up from behind my back. These dug deeper into my vulnerable scar. Perhaps it didn't bother her as much as it did me, but it was painful nonetheless.

The scar hurt me in many different ways, and the wound festered because of my family's silence. It hurts the most from the realization that I had been coddled over the years. Though I have tried to wean myself from it, I still feel immature sometimes. At different points in the past years I've both enjoyed and agonized in the fact that I am the youngest. The good feeling has been from being able to look up and to learn from what Joy was the first to do in our household. However, at times I've also felt totally helpless and incapable of being independent, taking risks, learning from my mistakes, and so grow up. All these scars have been coupled with the guilt of feeling favored and protected.

Perhaps I've never been favored after all and I've blown it out of proportion. But there have been little hints dropped here and there, and this stinging hurt tells me the problem still exists. I am unsure of whether anything I think or feel about this has any merit, because so little has been said in the open.

Once again, there's another confrontation building between Joy and me. She criticizes my primitive drawings, and feeling jealous, I scribble on her paper. Mom hears of it, and Joy takes yet another lambasting, while I escape unscathed. I still wonder what it would have been like to be the eldest.

~*"My Scar,"* excerpt from a seventh grade journal by Frank Jiles. [5]

Working harmoniously together, with everybody contributing, establishes an appreciation for everyone in the family. Family order can be helped by assigning age-appropriate chores to members of the household, making sure that people are personally doing things for themselves (making a bed, picking up clothes, making lunch, doing homework), and also contributing to the care of the household community (helping with laundry, setting the table, reading to younger ones, emptying garbage, stacking wood, working in the yard or garden). Children are praised for their own self-care, which is important, but the care of others in the community nourishes and helps to create a balanced atmosphere of giving and receiving.

At The Well we sought to further personal and community responsibility. Student jobs at school were an integral part of our community because they developed responsibility and established an avenue for the cycle of giving and receiving. These chores changed with the seasons. In the winter, students shoveled snow and used the snow blowers to open up the school and skating areas. If the roads were icy, students helped to shovel sand on the road before school. Singing, laughing, and shoveling in the crisp, early morning air sets a pretty healthy atmosphere for the day. We felt a lot of pride in our students, and enjoyed a camaraderie with them working and playing together. Having kids notice and do what needed to be done without being asked, created a huge sense of respect that we felt for our own children and the students at The Well. To witness the state of chaos of the school at 2:55 p.m., having been lived and worked in for the past eight hours, and then to see total order restored between 3:00 and 3:20 – as students vacuumed, cleaned, fed animals, cleaned stalls, cleaned bathrooms, and reorganized cubbies – let us witness or participate in a small miracle each day.

Family meetings and conferences served as a useful venue for discussing different roles in the family. Parents can be the last to realize how capable their children are, so a list of age-appropriate chores and expectations for the different age groups were discussed at parent conferences on a regular basis.

The spring of 1976 was a time of construction all around us. While the Whitehouses began building on the hill, we were clearing for a pond, as well as continuing to clear for a large soccer field, and we also decided to build a barn. For many years, our little goat shed had served as horse stable, hen house, sheep shed, and bunny hutch, housing the much-loved school animals.

Kambrah had dreamed of a horse of her own while caring for years for the many school animals shared by all. With a larger barn, she could realize her dream and have her own horse, so we decided to build. Roger, Jay's brother, agreed to be the foreman, and Jay, Ak (12 years old), Kambrah (14 years old), and I were the crew. Danda, too young to really do too much, helped when there was something for her to do, but mostly played with friends and her cousin around the barn construction.

Jay and Rog' got together one evening, found a gallon cardboard milk carton, squished it into different shapes, and came up with a form they liked, a gambrel-roofed barn. That was it! Perfect dimensions for the barn structure, as it turned out.

That spring, the hole for the foundation was dug, the cement walls were poured, and we were ready to start building as soon as school was out.

They go to the forest for palm or pine,
the stuff for the humbler homes;
The mountain gives up its valued
gifts for stately spires and domes;
But whether they work with marble or sod,
the builder is hand and hand with God.

~William Dunbar [6]

The Whitehouse family moved into the schoolhouse separate from our house for the summer, creating out of a number of classrooms an incredibly cozy home. Carol had the ability to make even a motel room an extension of their home, providing a feeling of safety, coziness, and permanence – if just for one night.

Build we did, every day, all summer long as simultaneously the Whitehouses were building their house on the hill. A barn is a great project. The construction of the frame gratifies the need to see immediate progress. Pounding nails has to be one of the best forms of therapy. When it comes to nailing, builders today seem to be more in the vein of Rambo, or someone carrying an Uzi in the form of a nail gun, wandering around on the construction site rat-a-tat-tatting and spraying their nails into the woodwork. The challenge of hammering a nail in, with as few strokes as possible, and not leaving an "elephant print," was one that presented itself daily that summer. And somehow, the wielding of the hammer must have regularly cleared the satanic energy from our brain, leaving us exhausted, but in great spirits at the end of the day.

As a work crew, our spirits were consistently high. The obvious progress each day energized us and kept us going. Kambrah and Ak were amazingly competent builders. At the time, I took for granted what good workers our kids were, how skillful they were, and how much fun they were to work with. Now I realize we were truly blessed to have such willing and able cohorts.

Patience is power; with time and patience the mulberry leaf becomes silk.

~Chinese Proverb

We didn't start at the crack of dawn each day, as most construction crews do. I don't believe Roger, our fearless leader, had ever seen the crack of dawn, unless he saw it after he had been driving all night to go sailing. He was the type of person who seemed to live in slow motion, but accomplished wonders. We would gather at a leisurely 9:00 a.m. – after all, it was summer. We worked until there was a hitch in the understanding of the construction plans, and that meant break time. Rog would step back, groan as he sat on his haunches, pencil in hand, take a deep breath and sigh, look over the problem, chewing on his tongue as it made a walnut-sized protrusion rotating in his left cheek (many a Garland male chewed their tongue... indicating deep thought... ahem... and a peculiar gene thread). At last, Roger would take out his flame-throwing Zippo lighter and light up a cigarette. He'd inhale, holding the smoke in his lungs and mouth for what seemed an inordinate amount of time, look over the problem area again, finally exhale a huge volume of smoke and say, "Uh," and think some more. The "uh" was like an icon on a computer monitor, found in the upper right hand corner of the screen, that turns around indicating that the computer is finding some information on the Internet for you, and "not to worry" if you can't see anything happening. Sometimes the "Uh" would engage me for a longer period of time than I had mentally bargained for, so the wait became a test of patience on my part. This process was so predictable that both Kambrah and Ak would stand behind Roger, both of them looking at the problem, and mime the chewing of the tongue, the lighting of the cigarette, inhaling, holding, and finally letting go, right down to the perfectly timed "Uh," although no sound was uttered on their part. Then they'd burst out laughing. We all would.

Of course, no one but Roger could solve the problem. Roger was a master at finding solutions, be it building a building, fixing a car, or repairing any kind of machinery. Somehow, suddenly, something would appear on his inner screen and he'd have the answer. Looking back, his patience with us was way beyond the call of duty to family, or anything else.

If I cannot be free, To do such work as pleases me,
Near woodland pools and under trees, You'll get no work at all; for I
Would rather live this life and die A beggar or a thief,
Than be a working slave with no days free.

~William H. Davies, (1871-1940) 7

Our spirits remained high, working into the late afternoon, taking time for swim breaks, until the latter part of August. Then our enthusiasm began to flag. Well, Kambrah's, Ak's, and mine did. Summer was slipping by, and no days off seemed to be in view. The notion of entitlement crept into my psyche. I felt we deserved a few lazy days at the lake, time to wonder what to do, reading in the daytime, playing cards or Cosmic Whimpout.

But we still had stalls to build, and the board and batten on the outside of the barn needed completing. Fortunately, the roof was done, and that was a mercy. Today, I look at the height of those trusses and wonder how any one of us got up there to nail plywood and shingle the roof. At the time, we laughed and enjoyed the fun while we yammered and hammered away. I must say that when Rog yanked my ladder over so I could reach the next shingle better, I found myself wrapped around the top rungs like an orangutan, my breath coming in gasps, and not immediately seeing the humor as readily as he did. But that was earlier in the summer.

We – Kambrah, Ak, and I – began to drag more and more, and then to lobby for some vacation time. We met as a family, the three children, Jay, and I at the dining room table, four of us hoping to come up with an end-of-summer vacation time. I did whine, I have to admit, pointing out the necessity of lake time during the day, not just at the end of it. (We all did swim and picnic at the end of many of the days.) I made a great case for how hard we had worked, how good-naturedly we met each day. All the while undermining the completion of the project, I blabbed on. Jay, on the other hand, reminded us of our agreement and goal that committed us to build a barn, and complete it.

When work is a pleasure,
Life is a joy!
When work is a duty,
Life is slavery!

~Maxim Gorky, *The Lower Depths, 1903* [8]

All work and no rest takes the spring and bound out of the most vigorous life. Time spent resting is not time wasted but time gained.

~M.B.Grier [9]

Part of the agreement involved building the barn cheerily, which felt far from the mood in the room. Quiet and sullen would probably better depict the atmosphere. We were stuck. No one moved. No one spoke. Silently, and I must say extremely irritatingly, Jay got up and left the house for the barn, to start the day's work. "Martyr," I thought. "Tunnel-visioned, goal-oriented so-and-so." The three of us remained silently seated at the long, pine, dining-room table. Slowly, we rose to head for the barn, dragging along. I don't know who it was, Kambrah or Ak, but one of them started singing some work song, something like, "Oh... Freedom," making the rest of us laugh and join in, "And before I'd be a slave...." not in a nice way, but in a manner that was both sarcastic, "...I'd be buried in my grave...." and quite a bit over the top. However, and I'm not able to say just when a transformation took place, we were suddenly not only really singing, (not before Jay and Roger had taken note of the sarcasm), but also we were working along at a good clip, and once again reveling in the progress. Singing at that moment became like praying for one's enemies: it started off tongue in cheek, and then without realizing the exact time, at some point, in the midst of it, we were released from the ill feeling that had paralyzed our hearts and slowed our feet.

Some men give up their designs when they have almost reached the goal; while others, on the contrary, obtain a victory by exerting, at the last moment, more vigorous efforts than before.

~Polybius [10]

As far as our dispute as to how to fill the last days of summer, Jay and I both held valid positions. I wanted vacation time, which afforded relaxation (something we seldom did as a family) and, best of all, from my point of view, instant gratification. His view of completion presented closure and fulfilling a commitment, and delayed the gratification. In the end, I was grateful for his follow through. I know it's very difficult to be the hard-nose in the group. It is always such a delicate balance.

An enterprise when fairly once begun, Should not be left till all that ought is won.

~William Shakespeare [11]

Jay was able to supply the example of discipline and force for the students at school, as well as for the members of our family. His perseverance and energy allowed people to realize they could accomplish anything they wanted to do. Quite an amazing gift to have in our midst, and, most of the time, I appreciated the characteristic.

We did finish the barn before school started that fall, and we rejoiced at the accomplishment. We felt a tremendous collective pride at its completion. To this day, I marvel at our kids for what they were able to do, and the fun it was for Jay and me to have built the barn with them, and with Roger. I felt totally grateful for the experience, and once again very "Lucky."

The reward of a thing well done is having it done.

~Ralph Waldo Emerson [12]

We filled the loft area with hay, the five stalls were quickly filled with horses and a donkey, and the ground level, or basement area, designed to house sheep and goats, actually became the home of tools, lawn mowers, and snow blowers.

NOTES:

Chapter 9: A Family Visit to Toni's Dad

by Toni Garland

In the spring of 1978, I realized that I had neglected to foster a relationship between our children and my dad, their grandfather. (It had only taken 16 years to come to this realization.) Gaining the understanding, through history, that roots and heritage are important parts of us, nevertheless, I simply had failed to make time for our kids to even meet their grandfather.

My dad had moved to California and remarried when I was in high school, leaving my mother to fend for herself and educate three children, which in fact she did. She probably had far more peace of mind doing it after his departure, although at times it was a difficult and lonely job. My father had tons of energy and lots of humor, along with being an out-of-sight, out-of-mind sort of guy. He moved from our New York family into his new life and to his California family and never looked back, at least as far as I could tell. We spoke often on the phone over the years, mostly with me listening to off-color jokes, or descriptions of his latest business deal. He always invited us to come and visit, but neither he nor I made the effort. Our phone contact seemed to fulfill what our father-daughter relationship needed.

In any case, I knew he would be thrilled if we planned a trip out West and visited with him. I realized only my effort, and mine alone, would bring about a reunion. I had the greater motivation, since I saw the importance in children meeting and knowing their grandfather.

I mentioned the idea to Jay, who was totally unenthusiastic, hating to give up good summer time to travel. Charlie Willard and his backhoe were just completing the construction of pond at The Well, and landscaping and seeding the pond hill should be done, at the proper time, so that the banks of the pond wouldn't erode. Never-ending projects were always good reasons to remain at home for Jay.

All travel has its advantages. If the traveler visits better countries, he may learn to improve his own; and if fortune carries him to worse, he may learn to enjoy his own.

~Johnson [1]

I countered vehemently that we had never taken a vacation away with our family, save a week or so on Cape Cod. That isn't to say that we didn't hike, swim, and camp – we did. However, it was all done right here in New Hampshire, and we loved it.

As children, neither Jay nor I came from vacationing families. Visiting relatives in the summertime was the most important and wonderful time of the year for me, incorporating swimming and fishing, cousins, aunts, uncles, and grandparents into the lazy days of summer, but I saw it more as visiting family and less as vacation. In Jay's family, even that did not occur. Neither his father, the family black sheep, nor his mother, a sort of "Cinderella" with a wicked stepmother in Germany, had any desire to visit their relatives or their childhood haunts.

I wonder now what we could have been thinking not to take a vacation with the kids in all those years. Actually, at the time, we thought, "Vacation? Who needs a vacation! Here we are, in the most beautiful vacationland of all. Why go somewhere else? And, "If you live your life in a balanced way, no one needs a vacation. Kids need time at home to be on their own, time to dream up their own activities, time to think." There were probably many more reasons as well.

All of the above is true, but really, think about it! Who leads a balanced life? Not the Garlands, that was for sure. Working on projects tipped the balance scales most certainly. Varied definitely, but balanced? Never! Did I love it? Of course I did. Certainly, New Hampshire is a vacationland: breathtakingly beautiful, but what makes it a "vacationland" is that the people are coming from somewhere else, out of their set routines, away from their everyday diversions. Kids do need time to plan their own activities, and if you don't believe it, just hang out with a child that is out of practice, or who has never had to entertain herself for any length of time. The thing he or she is good at is putting pressure on the adult to "make something happen." Summer vacation for teachers is a long time; we could have both. Why go somewhere else? Well, obviously, to broaden horizons and experience new things, but mostly to be together as a family unit, without diversions and interruption. Seeing the country and my father became a priority with me. This vacation idea took front and center; I was determined to go.

Jay did agree to go, somewhat reluctantly. As time wore on, however, he really got into the idea. The next thing I knew, he had the entire trip planned.

We camped along the way, stopping at some awesomely beautiful sites, and also at some real pits. Ak, often on the CB (they were popular at the time), kept us on track, finding campsites or gas stations. Every time I got on the darn thing, I'd get nervous, so it didn't hold much appeal for me. Sometimes, we were high up on a mountainside, off by ourselves watching a magnificent sunset. The Black Hills of South Dakota was holy countryside. Montana, particularly West Yellowstone, where we spent time at our friend

Katy's ranch, made one realize why Westerners felt claustrophobic in the East. The huge expanse of azure sky, bordered by the Rockies, expanded not only our visual horizons, but released our emotions of limitations, letting the breath flow freer and deeper.

Colorado offered remarkable skies and sunsets. On the other hand, an RV campground in Arizona was an all-time low. Our tents were located on hardpan between two RVs that huffed and puffed all night, screen doors slamming and TVs blaring. It was so bad, it was comical. It was hard to imagine we were even camping. None of us got any sleep, but we did laugh a lot.

We had the habit of driving too long each day, becoming in the end desperate for a place to stay, patience setting with the sun, and irritability rising as someone on the CB guided us to our unknown resting place, which was always a surprise, not always a pleasant one.

Neither Jay nor I had investigated those activities that might appeal to the kids, such as rafting, or hiking, or biking. We didn't take advantage physically of the "land," except for camping on it and swimming at each opportunity. Of course, there was plenty to do on our friend's ranch: riding, fishing, and hiking. Montana was incredibly beautiful. Yellowstone National Park had its own wonders to offer, but outside of the park, the landscape was breathtaking, too. After a week of cards in the evening, long talks in the night, horseback riding, taking in a rodeo, and general living together, we were off to Southern California, the land of sunshine and oranges – and my father.

I loved both driving and being a passenger. Of the five of us, I was the only one who really liked both, so I was somewhat blinded as to how unpopular "just riding" was for the rest of the family, never to be fully enlightened until years later. Off the beaten track has always appealed to me; finding out what is over the hill or around the corner "Just to see" intrigues me, whether riding or hiking. Getting lost on vacation has never been upsetting to me, unless there is a time constriction or other people are worried. None of these side trips appealed to the rest of the family. In fact, fear and apprehension were the results in some cases, if things didn't roll right along as planned.

We traveled on to California, taking in the Grand Canyon, Bryce Canyon, and Zion National Park. Jay is sure we stopped at every site there was to see in the West, taking in endless places. My memory is of flying by at 90 miles an hour, the brown highway signs indicating historical spots or sites, with me remarking, "That looks interesting!" and hearing a grunt of agreement from the rest of the family as we accelerated past them and on our way.

We spent a week or so in Irvine, where my dad and his family lived. My father, comfortable with our "out-of-sight, out-of-mind" kind of relationships, changed once we were within sight. He then focused 100 percent of his attention on us. Actually, that focus was tough to take for more than a week; hence, I realized the value of the phone relationship. In looking at it now, I'm sure that the continent between my dad and me afforded us both the space we needed.

It is the duty of the host to make his guests feel at home. It is the duty of the guests to remember that they are not.

~A Sign at the entrance of an English castle open to the public.

I was thrilled to have our children meet my dad and have some firsthand experience with their grandfather. I think for Kambrah and Ak, it was their only time with him; Danda was to spend another couple of weeks in California with him a few years later. My dad adored Danda; it was love at first sight. Danda generally had the wit and courage to say what she was thinking and had a "no frills" attitude towards life. My dad loved her directness. Later, he begged me to have her come for another visit.

Visits should be short like a winter's day, lest you're too troublesome, hasten away.

~Ben Franklin [2]

My father was a 24/7 kind of companion, laughing and joking throughout our sightseeing, although his mobility was somewhat impaired by an ankle that was still healing from a break. Yet, we all huffed to keep up with him. We did just about all the sightseeing that the Irvine, California area had to offer. So much so that by the final hours in Disneyland, the kids began hiding their tickets so that they wouldn't have to go on another ride.

Grandparents – Jay's folks and my mom – had, over the years, played such important roles in our children's lives, yet when I look back, the two weeks that our kids spent with my dad seemed more than adequate. I'm sure they saw him at his best. They never witnessed his heavy drinking, or loss of temper. I'm sure he lost out not seeing them grow and mature and experiencing what great grandkids he had, but we all make our choices.

Knowing your roots, if at all possible, offers a huge advantage in expanding one's identity. I was grateful we took that opportunity, however small a window; it was large enough for me. I hope it was for the kids.

On our return trip, the Mojave Desert was the low point, crossing in midday, no air-conditioning, windows rolled down allowing the hot air to circulate, air that seemed directly vented from a blast furnace. Danda was so hot and uncomfortable she cried!

"Aw, Danda. Stop crying. Crying only increases your heat and discomfort," we all chimed in, next to tears of discomfort ourselves. She only cried harder. There was no way to comfort each other. The temperature made it too hot for us to touch; our voices were rasping and less than consoling. We were all red-faced and panting, scarfing up huge paper cups of ice that we had gotten at the one and only gas station along the way. Nowadays, kids are riding in vans with air-conditioning and movies or videos to keep them occupied. With climate control, one needn't even know one is in the desert.

The kids and Jay could hardly wait to get home. The blast of the fresh, green fragrance when we were returning east and had crossed the Mississippi River filled our lungs and urged us homeward. (One other time I experienced that amazing fragrance of green plant life, which one can take for granted, was when we deplaned in Fairbanks, Alaska after two years on the tundra in Barrow.) Ak could hardly wait to get home and mow the grass – home, and the familiar, being of the utmost importance to him at that time in his life. Having seen amazingly beautiful places on our sojourn, we were all heartened to see that in no way did those magnificent places out-shine New Hampshire. That, I guess, is the nature of home.

Now, years later, I regret our ineptitude as parents at executing a good vacation, and am aware of the importance of learning how to vacation together. That is, the importance of learning how to relax together. Families need that time to create new avenues of connection, undisturbed by outside influences. Visiting places that are new to everyone levels the playing field, and allows all involved an opportunity to be first-time explorers together.

After we returned from "out West," summer quickly turned into business as usual: lake time, landscaping the pond hill, and preparing for school in the fall.

The best part of a journey is coming back home.

~E. Annie Proulx [3]

NOTES:

CHAPTER 10: THE WHITEHOUSES AT THE WELL

BY TONI GARLAND

In 1976, our friends Brooks and Carol Whitehouse decided to build a home up on the hill close behind our house and the school buildings. Because of the national energy crisis and the uncertainty of the world (what has changed?), their move was an attempt to share their resources and energies with those of our family and The Well. Jay and I had been cutting trees for firewood up on the knoll by our house on weekends since 1970, so there was a small clearing already started. Once decided upon, we were all impatient to get started. Carol had been teaching at The Well for a number of years, and their four children had all attended the school. Some were still students at our school. Brooks Sr. liked to have things done yesterday. He had their beautiful house on Condy Hill in Peterborough on the market and sold before an eye could wink. The buyer required they vacate their house before the new house, designed by Jay's brother Peter, could be completed.

We became more and more excited about the Whitehouses becoming close neighbors. Since Carol was teaching fifth and sixth grade, she was already involved in every aspect of the school. Moving closer made sharing lives, jobs, children, love, and energy easier.

So, in June, after school was out, Carol, Brooks, and their family took up temporary residence in the Upper Building classrooms.

When September arrived with school opening at hand, the need for their family to relinquish the Upper Building to grades five through eight became imminent. So, the Whitehouses moved into our house. Son Brooks bunked with Ak in his room. Daughters Julie and Ann were in college, and Liz was in Italy. Daughter Cilla was down at the end of the hall with Danda, next to Kambrah's room. We all settled in. A surprisingly smooth beginning of school was also a tremendous boon. With all of us either working or in school, the weeks developed an easy rhythm. Brooks Sr. was off early to Boston each morning, and Carol, Jay, and I were teaching at The Well. Our daily school routines probably contributed to the ease of living together; the exact magic ingredient that really made the two households work together still remains a mystery. Nowadays, I suspect the hand of Spirit was at work. Happily grateful, we all knew somewhere inside us that both families were totally blessed.

Kambrah and Brooks had graduated from The Well and entered the tenth grade in the local high school that fall. Their entering public school was a huge step. I can still see them in my mind's eye, that first day of school, cautiously walking across the lawn together in jeans, book bags slung over their shoulders. I cried unexpectedly, realizing it was the end of an era. I wasn't quite sure what was ending, but I knew Kambrah was moving further out. Yet, independence was what I most sought for our children. Since this was Carol's third child to go off to high school, she was able to offer me a strong shoulder to lean on. Most parents experience this kind of sadness much earlier in their child's life when they put their first grader on the big yellow school bus. My yellow bus experience was somewhat delayed, and my tears came as a total surprise.

Children do not know how their parents love them, and they never will till the grave closes over the parents, or till they have children of their own.

~Cooke [1]

I learned many things while living together with the Whitehouses, not the least of which was appreciation. You cannot believe the pleasure it gives when someone not only notices, but also appreciates and thanks you for a job that you have done regularly for 18 years, which has otherwise gone unnoticed or unacknowledged. Carol and I were genuinely grateful for each and every task that the other performed. It sounds ridiculous, but it is nevertheless true. Imagine going to the laundry room and finding things already folded, or to the dishwasher and it's empty! Imagine a vacuumed dining room after dinner. Yup, Brooks often did that. Of course, there was twice as much work to do, but the actual doing of it seemed to take one-quarter the time. This came at the end of a jam-packed, very full academic fall, so you know things went well. We even had two other school children staying with us during a part of this period because their parents were busy reorganizing a failing business and needed a place for their children while they revived the source of their livelihood. These kids, by the way, had chicken pox during their stay with us, along with two of ours.

The foolish man seeks happiness in the distance; the wise grows it under his feet.

~James Oppenheim [2]

Each week, Carol and I would agree that it would be nice to invite people over for dinner. I don't think we ever did, unless it was for huge family Sunday dinners. The weeks zoomed by so fast that Thursdays came unexpectedly. Carol and I would go shopping for mountains of food and return home with the car crammed with groceries. Jay's trick (developed that fall) of leaning on the horn at the foot of the driveway, rallying everyone to the porch, readying themselves to unload and stash the food, brought people from all over the place. To this day, the mention of this particular technique has some members of the immediate family nuts with irritation. Everybody helped unload the bags from the car. We'd cook dinner while the kids played music; then we'd eat. After dinner, all of us would wind up in the living room telling stories of the day and having backrubs and foot massages. Homework followed, stories were read to Danda, 14 drinks of water were filled for Cilla, the youngest Whitehouse, and then the house became soft and quiet as everyone else did homework or practiced an instrument. The rich tones of young Brooks' cello wafted through the house as he practiced; Ak practiced James Taylor's latest tunes on his guitar. I loved to hear live music in the house, so of course the practicing was another welcomed bonus of our temporary, communal set-up. Saturdays came around, and we worked outside, cutting, clearing, and stacking endless piles of wood

Jay seldom finished a project before he was formulating plans for the next one, which held true in the case of the barn as well. Before the last nail was hammered into the last batten, we were clearing a wet and rocky depression – consisting of dead elms, live hardwoods, and many large boulders – for a future pond. The never-ending project of clearing for a full-sized soccer field was also ongoing.

We did hire some people to help cut trees and clear the future pond area. The hiring of someone else to do work that we could do ourselves, an almost unheard of idea in the Garland household, in this case saved quite a few backs. Those amazing woodcutters felled, limbed, and cut tree trunks into four-foot sections, employing gigantic chainsaws with a speed that defied reality. I had thought we were all pretty efficient with chainsaws until I saw how those woodcutters operated

Hard work spotlights the character of people; some turn up their sleeves, some turn up their nose, and some don't turn up.

~Sam Ewing [3]

The whole school helped clear the pond area at different times during the fall, and our families continued on the weekends. We cut and moved a lot of wood that fall, as we did every fall.

We always had Parents' Supper the Friday night before Wood Day. I would cook a pot of some mixture – lasagna, curried chicken and rice, or the like, something that fed multitudes – and the faculty put together a huge salad and brought in prize-winning homemade desserts. Always, there was great bread, fresh cider, and a lot of wine. I think the wine, candles, and fires burning in the four brick fireplaces were key to the success of the evening. (Candles improved all of our dinners, so we usually had them going at any opportunity.) We all cleaned beforehand, and transformed the classrooms in the house into candle-lit dining rooms, with beautiful fall flowers and brilliant leaves for centerpieces. Once again, Indian bedspreads became tablecloths. Parents' Supper was the only event of the year when children weren't invited: only adult family members, aunts, uncles, and grandparents. After the dishes were done and most of the guests had gone home, the faculty gathered in the living room for more dessert, wine, relaxation, and a good deal of laughter. I must say, our faculty always had a great sense of humor.

Wood Day followed the next day. Parents, children, and faculty came once again with chainsaws, trucks, wood splitters, and malls. While parents cut wood, kids piled brush, rode the trucks, split, and stacked wood. Forty cords were brought in that day. Then, after lunch, we played soccer at the Peterborough playground in the afternoon. Looking back, I shake my head and wonder where the energy came from. We worked and played, rain or shine.

One year, the puddles were plentiful on the playground. We'd race down the field, slipping and sliding, the ball coming to a sudden stop in the middle of a puddle. L.T., one of the parents, hot on the soccer ball's track, didn't come to a sudden stop, slid into the puddle face first, and then came to a stop on the other side. I can still see him, regaining his feet, carefully unfolding his body, adjusting his mud-splashed glasses, and looking very much like the monster from the lost lagoon. I think Sue, our first-and second-grade teacher, lost the use of two of her fingers for a period of time in that particular game. It was a slippery one.

With Carol and Brooks as neighbors, friends, and colleagues, care of each other, hard work, and dedication was truly enhanced at The Well.

After the completion of the barn, that fall, Roger began to build a house for Ursula, Jay's mother. Locating her home at the end of the little soccer field near the main house just felt right, making her available to us all, but giving her the privacy she required. Probably there exists in the Garland gene pool a gene for organizing one project to follow rapidly on the heels of the next. Roger seemed to have the same motivation as Jay when it came to keeping things moving in the building department.

Ursula had been widowed for two years, and no longer enjoyed living on her beautiful farm at the end of a dirt road in New Ipswich, an even-smaller village than Peterborough. When she and Jay's father had moved there originally, the end-of-a-dirt-road location afforded them the privacy they were seeking. But, as a widow, privacy turned into isolation. We looked all over town for a nice little house, but none really appealed to her. Jay decided to give her a piece of our property, Jay's brother Peter designed the perfect "Grandmother's Cottage," and Roger and his wife Barbara built the house. They worked on it that year, and she moved into it the following spring. She loved her new home, and who wouldn't? It was a beautiful design, so well thought out for her needs.

Ursula's home was a two-minute walk from ours. Because of the proximity, Ursula was able to live there, alone, until she was 95 – for all but the last month of her life. With her so close, we could walk to see her each day, have coffee, yak, have a power-nap on her cozy window seat, read, and come home. Having her next door meant more spur-of-the moment adventures, as well, something we both enjoyed.

Large Sunday dinners at Ursula's were not as frequent after she moved next door; I suppose seeing her daily took the edge off the need for a huge Sunday gathering on her part. Also, she was getting older, and cooking huge Sunday dinners for 25 does take some effort, even if you're an expert.

With Ursula living at the end of the little soccer field, and the Whitehouses living in their new home up on the knoll, and the new barn filled with horses – Cilla's, Kambrah's, and three school horses, plus a donkey – our little community began to settle into a new rhythm, with a stability that we thoroughly enjoyed. Our kids met the Whitehouse kids at the barn early each morning to do chores, before going off to school. Carol and I often met for tea in the afternoon to catch up on the day of classes and children, hopes and fears.

Very shortly after moving into their home, the Whitehouses generously shared their new house with the school for reading groups. At 7:30 a.m., fifth and sixth graders trudged up the hill to Carol's for their first-period reading class. There, they were greeted by Carol and Peggy Brown, another fabulous teacher and parent. With teacups in hand, the adults chatted, joked, exchanged news, and planned the day. Then everyone settled into comfortable seats and quieted down in order to read and discuss stories together. The children were provided with an academic atmosphere, but one couched in friendship, love, granola snacks, doughnuts, and cozy fires made in the early morning by Brooks Sr. – one in the big brick fireplace in the living room, the other in the little Jötul wood stove on the glassed-in porch, where one of the reading groups met.

The supreme happiness of life is the conviction that we are loved.

~Victor Hugo, *Les Miserables, 1862* 4

For a period of time, the study in Brooks' and Carol's home was altered to become a bedroom for Brooks' ailing mother, who had recently lost her leg to cancer. The room was complete with hospital bed and newly plumbed sink. Mrs. Whitehouse (Ann) held court each morning propped up in bed with cozy, downy pillows, ensconced in the comfort and safety that Brooks and Carol knew how to provide so well. She greeted the children as they stopped to say good morning before class. How lucky she was to have the children arrive with good morning cheer, and how lucky were those kids to be having class in the midst of a life of a family full of love and care. They didn't just read about it, they witnessed and participated in it.

Later, the two grades were divided into three reading groups. Anne Marie, a remarkable teacher and a parent of two boys at school, joined our staff, bringing her marvelous open-ended questions and high expectations to the children, making them think deeply, resulting in their having a strong connection with the literature they were reading. The atmosphere remained consistently cozy and vibrant.

The first time I read an excellent work, it is to me just as if I had gained a new friend; and when I read over a book I have perused before, it resembles the meeting with an old one.

~Joel Goldsmith [5]

The children wept, became outraged, and trembled through *To Kill a Mocking Bird*, laughed and clucked through *The Dunn Cow*, and struggled with the constant human shortcomings of man portrayed in *The Bible*. Man just couldn't seem to get it straight, and kept doing just the opposite of what was expected. Of course, the wrath of God descended over and over. David, a student, would groan each time as he anticipated another "bad choice" on the part of the Israelites. "Will they ever get it together?" he'd sigh. Together, they experienced many wonderful and thought-provoking books. *Sir Gibbie, Otto of the Silver Hand, Robin Hood, A Proud Taste for Scarlet and Miniver, Swiftly Tilting Planet, A Wrinkle in Time, Wild Animals I Have Known, The Diary of Anne Frank*, and so many more. The material was rich; the discussions were even richer, as teachers and students were encouraged to share personal experiences that were related to the material. Excellent choices in literature abounded. The students' colorful illustrations of the book that they were currently reading brightened the walls of the school for Coffee Houses or poetry recitals, along with the paintings and linoleum prints produced from Ruth's art classes, which illustrated the older students' reading subjects.

To read without reflecting, is like eating without digesting.

~Burke [6]

Carol became an expert birder while teaching birding to the students at The Well. She began her own study with her students at school, developing her knowledge along with the children through listening to tapes, reading, and using bird identification books if unfamiliar birds landed on feeders strategically placed just outside the windows. Often, she invited students to spend the night at her house so they could rise before dawn for early morning bird walks, followed by treats at Nonie's, the local bakery and coffee shop, followed by classes.

New Hampshire's early-morning spring birding can be an "Outward Bound" experience, because of the cold, or the biting black flies that find shelter and food in one's nostrils, eyes, and ears, or the dampness. Coffee, hot chocolate, and grilled coffee sticks at the local bakery turned all of it into a luxurious memory. Nothing like the contrast of freezing toes and fingers from the outdoors, and burning tongues and lips from hot chocolate.

A few times, Carol was somewhat belittled by other "advanced birders" for her independent approach, not having a "certified professional" guide her course of study. Unflinchingly, she pursued her quest for knowledge, taking her students along with her every step of the way. Through her personal wonder of nature, her own intelligence, and her love of children, Carol influenced so many young people, offering them her incredible knowledge of the birds and love of nature. Once a child had experienced Carol's group, they scurried each spring to spot the first 50 birds, recording the sightings. Quite a few of her students still bird every spring, and they are now in their forties or fifties.

Nature is man's teacher. She unfolds her treasures to his search, unseals his eye, illumines his mind, and purifies his heart; an influence breathes from all the sights and sounds of her existence.

~Alfred Billings Street [7]

Ak, at nine, as a new birder, built Carol an enormous bird feeder that probably would have fed the entire Bronx Zoo aviary, so enthralled and grateful was he with this newfound field of nature. We were grateful that he felt so inspired. As a parent, each new field of interest with which one's child connects causes great appreciation.

Witnessing our children loving what they were doing inspired deep gratitude.

Teachers who learn along with their students create a new dynamic of energy, promoting a constant, two-way exchange of knowledge between the teachers and the students. Motivated children are so quick to learn, and have such amazing eyes and ears; often, they are the first to see wonders in the woods. When walking with children in nature class, Lauren found the antlers that I had overlooked—literally stepped over. During pond study, Danny found the caddis worm houses while I was completing the verbal description of them or offering a picture of what we were seeking. On the beach, it was Bonnie who spotted a sand dollar smaller than a fingertip. You can imagine how quickly the kids discerned the different features of a bird, noting size, shape, and coloring in a single glance, while I looked frantically in the book.

NOTES:

NOTES:

NOTES

(Author's note: The citations in *Naked Education,* Books I through VI vary in their scope of attribution. For the past three decades we have collected quotes from many of our favorite authors and as well as from many collected works of quotations – several of which did not provide as much information as possible about each quotation in each of these six books, and we apologize for any missing citations. – Jay and Toni Garland)

Notes on Introduction: What is Naked Education?

1. Eli Jaxon-Bear, *Sudden Awakening;* (Tiburon, CA; New World Library, 2004)

2. *The Holy Bible*: King James Version Study Version; (Grand Rapids, MI; Zondervan Publishing; (John 14:2) 2010)

3. Kahlil Gibran; *The Prophet*; "On Children,"(NY, NY: Alfred A. Knopf, 1923)

4. Hafiz, *The Gift;* (New York, NY The Penguin Group, 1999)

5. Jay Garland, unpublished poem

6. from an Abraham-Hicks workshop

7. Ernest Holmes, *Creative Mind and Succes;* (Radford, VA, Wilder Publication, 2007)

8. *Holy Bible*: King James Version; Study Version; (Grand Rapids, MI: Zondervan Publishers; Ephesians 5:13, 2010)

9. William Blake, *Jerusalem*; (London, England: Forgotten Books, 2017)

10. Albert Einstein

11. Dr. Franz Hartmann

12. Henry David Thoreau, *The Writings of Henry David Thoreau*

13. Jane Austin, *Pride and Prejudice*

14. Henry Ward Beecher, *Life Thoughts*

15. Pablo Picasso, painter

16. Neville Goddard, *Your Faith is Your Fortune*; (Seaside, OR, Rough Draft Printing, 2011)

17. *The Gospel of Thomas*: the Gnostic Wisdom of Jesus; (Woodstock, Vermont; Skylight Paths Publishing, 2006)

Notes on Chapter 1: Ideas from Book 1

1. Carl Jung

2. Shakespeare

3. Joseph Campbell, *The Power of Myth;* (New York, NY; Anchor Books, *2017*)

4. A. J. Krishnamurti, *Think on These Things*

Notes on Chapter 2: The Challenge of Consciousness in Education

1. Robert Frost

2. Aldous Huxley

3. Joseph Campbell, *The Power of Myth;* (New York, NY; Anchor Books, *2017*)

4. Thornton Wilder

5. Carl Jung, *Development on the Personality, Volume 17 in the Collected Works of C.G. Jung; Princton/Bollingen Press; Princeton, NJ, Princton/Bollingen Press 1964)*

6. Soren Kierkegaard, *Either/Or*

7. Sai Baba

8. Henry Miller

9. Edith Hamilton

10. Samuel Coleridge

11. William Wadsworth

12. Julian Huxley, *Religion Without Revelation*

13. Albert Szent-Gyorgi

14. Johann Wolfgang von Goethe

15. Longchenpa

16. Hafiz of Shiraz

17. Eckhart Tolle, *The Power of Now*

18. *Holy Bible*: King James Version; Study Version; (Grand Rapid, MI, Zondervan Publishers 2000)

19. Rev. Joseph Running Wolf Sparti

20. Basho

21. John Gatto, *The Underground History of American Education*; (New York, NY; Oxford Village Press 2001)

22. Calvin Hall and Vernon Nordby; *A Primer of Jungian Psychology*

23. Carl Jung, *Psychological Types*

24. Ranier Maria Rilke

25. Emily Dickinson, *The Complete Poems of Emily Dickinson;* (New York, NY; Thomas H. Johnson, editor, Back Bay Books 1967)

26. Rudyard Kipling

27. Raoul Plus, *Living with God*

28. Tennyson

29. William Blake; *The Marriage of Heaven and Hell*

30. William Shakespeare

31. Marcus Aurelius

32. Robert Louis Stevenson

33. Johann Wolfgang Goethe

34. Seneca

35. William James

36. Sarah Bernhardt

37. Andrea Sarto

Notes on Chapter 3: The Role of Drama

1. Edna St. Vincent Millay, *Collected Poems*; edited my Norma Millay, (New York, NY: Harper Perennial, 1956)

2. Emily Dickinson, *The Complete Poems of Emily Dickinson* (New York, NY; Thomas H. Johnson, editor, Back Bay Books, 1976)

3. Showcase by Roy Newquist

4. Thomas Powers

5. John Keats; *The Complete Poems,* "Ode to a Grecian Urn" (New York, NY, Penguin Putnam, 1988)

6. Alexis Carrel, *Reflections of Life*

7 .D. William Hazlitt, *Criticism of Art*

8. Jay Garland, unpublished poem

9. Thomas Bailey Aldrech

Notes on Chapter 4: The Loss of Consciousness in Education

1. Leonardo Da Vinci

2. Alexander von Humboldt, *The Sphere and Duty of Government*

3. John Taylor Gatto, *The Underground History of American Education*; P.131-132, 2001, (New York, NY Oxford Village Press, 2001

4. Seneca

Notes on Chapter 6: The Rise and Demise of the High School

1. Fenelon

2. Jack Kornfield *The Art of Lovingkindness and Peace*

3. Buddha

4. Henry Wadsworth Longfellow

5. Jack Kornfield

6 .Ibsen

7. Tara Singh

8. J. Mason

9. Lydia H. Sigourney

10. Plato

11. Ken Carey

12. Bhagavad Gita

13. S.W. Temple

14. Euripides

15. Philip Toshio, Sudo, *Zen Guitar*

16. Amy Carmichael

17. Robert Frost, *Cluster of Faith*

18. Mark Twain

Notes on Chapter 7: Death of our Rock: Barley

1. H. W. Longfellow

2. Mark Twain, *Following the Equator*

3. Hillel the Elder

4. Arthur Miller

Notes for Chapter 8: Home and School Life

1. Alva Myrdal, Viola Klein, *Women's Two Roles;* (1956)

2. Jack Kornfield

3. Jade Snow Wong, Fifth Chinese Daughter; 1950

4. Sarah Hale, Traits of American Life (1835)

5. My Scar," excerpt from a seventh grade journal by Frank Jiles

6. William Dunbar

7. William H. Davies (1871-1940)

8. Maxim Gorky, *The Lower Depths,* 1903

9. M.B.Grier

10. Polybius

11. William Shakespeare

12. Ralph Waldo Emerson

Notes from Chapter 9: A Family Visit to Toni's Dad

1. Johnson

2. Ben Franklin

3. E. Annie Proulx

Notes from Chapter 10: The Whitehouses at The Well

1. Cooke

2. James Oppenheim

3. Sam Ewing

4. Victor Hugo *Les Miserables*, 1862

5. Joel Goldsmith

6. Burke

7.Alfred Billings Street

NOTES:

NOTES:

NOTES:

NOTES:

NOTES:

www.ingramcontent.com/pod-product-compliance
Lightning Source LLC
LaVergne TN
LVHW061259060426
835509LV00013B/1488